AFRICAN ETHNOGRAPHIC STUDIES OF THE 20TH CENTURY

Volume 79

SECTARIANISM IN SOUTHERN NYASALAND

SECTARIANISM IN SOUTHERN NYASALAND

R. L. WISHLADE

LONDON AND NEW YORK

First published in 1965 for the International African Institute by Oxford University Press.

This edition first published in 2018
by Routledge
2 Park Square, Milton Park, Abingdon, Oxon OX14 4RN

and by Routledge
711 Third Avenue, New York, NY 10017

Routledge is an imprint of the Taylor & Francis Group, an informa business

© 1965 International African Institute

All rights reserved. No part of this book may be reprinted or reproduced or utilised in any form or by any electronic, mechanical, or other means, now known or hereafter invented, including photocopying and recording, or in any information storage or retrieval system, without permission in writing from the publishers.

Trademark notice: Product or corporate names may be trademarks or registered trademarks, and are used only for identification and explanation without intent to infringe.

British Library Cataloguing in Publication Data
A catalogue record for this book is available from the British Library

ISBN: 978-0-8153-8713-8 (Set)
ISBN: 978-0-429-48813-9 (Set) (ebk)
ISBN: 978-1-138-60039-3 (Volume 79) (hbk)
ISBN: 978-0-429-47096-7 (Volume 79) (ebk)

Publisher's Note
The publisher has gone to great lengths to ensure the quality of this reprint but points out that some imperfections in the original copies may be apparent.

Disclaimer
The publisher has made every effort to trace copyright holders and would welcome correspondence from those they have been unable to trace.

SECTARIANISM IN SOUTHERN NYASALAND

R. L. WISHLADE

Published for the
INTERNATIONAL AFRICAN INSTITUTE
by the
OXFORD UNIVERSITY PRESS
LONDON   NEW YORK   IBADAN
1965

Oxford University Press, Amen House, London E.C.4

GLASGOW NEW YORK TORONTO MELBOURNE WELLINGTON
BOMBAY CALCUTTA MADRAS KARACHI LAHORE DACCA
CAPE TOWN SALISBURY NAIROBI IBADAN ACCRA
KUALA LUMPUR HONG KONG

© International African Institute, 1965

Printed in Great Britain by
W. & J. Mackay & Co. Ltd., Chatham, Kent

CONTENTS

		Page
	PREFACE	vii
I	INTRODUCTION	1
	The nature of sectarianism; ecological and social background	
II	THE ORIGINS OF THE SECTS	10
III	THE INCIDENCE AND EXTENT OF SECTARIANISM IN SOUTHERN NYASALAND	22
	Tribalism; the external connexions of the sects	
IV	DOCTRINES OF THE SECTS	35
	The White and simple secessionist sects; the Ethiopian Church: a synthetist sect	
V	RITUAL AND WORSHIP	53
	The weekly service; baptism; ritual associated with life crises: birth; marriage; death	
VI	THE OFFICIALS OF THE SECTS	62
	Deaconesses; deacons; elders; the local minister; the minister; the founder or head of the sect; the Ethiopian Church; the Roman Catholic hierarchy	
VII	THE ROLE OF SECT OFFICIALS IN NYASALAND SOCIAL LIFE	76
	The Ethiopian Church; the Nyasaland African National Congress; the Roman Catholic Church hierarchy	
VIII	THE SECT AS A SOCIAL GROUP	101
	Sects and local grouping; sects and kinship ties; the African sect's attraction for followers; social control in the sects; administration in the sects; sect economics; the sects' relations with outsiders	
IX	NYASALAND SECTARIANISM IN PERSPECTIVE—SOME COMPARISONS	129
	APPENDIX A. Analysis of the composition of households in part of Wendewende village containing the headquarters of the Faithful Church of Christ	145
	APPENDIX B. Poem forming the Introduction to a tract	156
	BIBLIOGRAPHY OF WORKS CITED IN THE TEXT	157
	INDEX	160

MAP

FIGURES AND TABLES

Map	Page
Southern Nyasaland	viii

Figures

1 The historical development of sects in Southern Nyasaland	13
2 Part of Wendewende village	145
3 Wendewende genealogy No. 1 (Cluster A)	146
4 Wendewende genealogy No. 2 (Cluster D)	149
5 Wendewende genealogy No. 3 (Cluster F)	151
6 Wendewende genealogy No. 4 (Cluster G)	152
7 Wendewende genealogy No. 5 (Cluster H)	154

Tables

I Number of pagans and Christians as obtained from field censuses	23
II The distribution of congregations in Mlanje	24
III Population increase 1931–1945	90

PREFACE

In 1958/59, when I carried out the fieldwork on which this book is based, Nyasaland was the scene of rapid social change. It has since become the independent state of Malawi. This particular change took place while this book was in the press, and the name by which the country was known at the time of this study has been retained.

I am particularly indebted to the many Africans, whose communities and churches are the subject of this book. I am grateful to them for much kindness and hospitality to me while I was living among them as well as for the guidance and information they so generously gave. I also wish to thank members of the British Colonial Service and missionaries working in the area, from whom I received much help and hospitality.

I wish here to acknowledge my gratitude to the International African Institute for the award of a Research Fellowship, which enabled me to undertake the fieldwork and a subsequent period of writing up, and in particular to the Administrative Director, Professor Daryll Forde, for his unfailing help in a variety of ways. I also owe a debt of gratitude to my teachers and colleagues in social anthropology for their comments on the earlier drafts of this book. The responsibility for any faults in it is of course mine and not theirs. Among those who helped me in one way or another in preparing for and carrying out this study, my thanks are especially due to: Dr. R. G. Abrahams, Dr. R. J. Apthorpe, Dr. G. Atkins, Dr. D. G. Bettison, Miss A. Currie, Che Duncan Kasombo, Mrs. M. Lyon, Rev. B. Malekebu, Dr. H. H. Meinhard, Dr. J. M. Middleton, Professor J. Clyde Mitchell, Dr. H. A. Powell, Rev. T. Price, Miss B. Pym, Dr. A. I. Richards, Rev. E. C. Severe, Dr. V. G. J. Sheddick, Professor G. Shepperson, Mr. B. Walker, Dr. P. Worsley.

R. L. WISHLADE

October 1964.

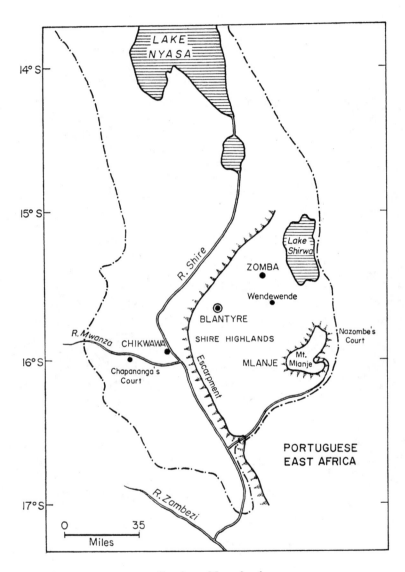

Southern Nyasaland

I

INTRODUCTION

The nature of sectarianism

ONE of the characteristics of the major world religions has been the process of sectarianism by which small new religious groups are formed by secession from existing groups. This differs from the establishment of a new religion inasmuch as the members of the new group, i.e. the sect, still consider themselves followers of the founder of the religion, although asserting their independence from other groups of followers. Sectarianism has been particularly characteristic of the history of Christianity, with the result that there are in the world today several thousand independent religious groups paying allegiance to Christ.

The mixing of peoples of different ethnic origins, as in the United States of America, and the advent of Christian missionaries to many parts of the world inhabited by pre-literate societies, have intensified the process of sectarianism in Christianity over the last century or so. Many new sects have been started by inhabitants of the areas to which missionaries have gone.

In Africa sectarianism is most marked in the Union of South Africa, where it was estimated in 1953 that there were about 2,000 Christian sects with an entirely African membership.[1] Here the number of sects appears to have risen roughly in a geometrical progression from 76 in 1918 to 320 in 1938 and 800 in 1948.[2] This seems to be the result not so much of an increase in their total membership as of constant splitting into smaller and smaller groups.[3]

Although nowhere else in Africa has sectarianism assumed such proportions, African sects have a wide distribution in many parts of the continent. Accounts of them have been written by missionaries, anthopologists, administrators, and others working in West, East, and Central Africa, as well as in the Union of South Africa.[4] My justification for adding to the already considerable literature on African sects is that I shall try to relate them fairly closely to the background of the social organization of the area in which they are found.

---

[1] Schlosser, 1958, p. 4.   [2] Ibid.   [3] Schlosser, op. cit., p. 10.
[4] A selection of these is to be found in the bibliography of this volume on pp. 157–9, and many are referred to in the text of the chapters which follow.

2 SECTARIANISM IN SOUTHERN NYASALAND

The first sect to be established by an African in Nyasaland was the Providence Industrial Mission started by John Chilembwe in 1900. Today there are more than thirty sects in the Southern Province of Nyasaland and it is with some of these that this book is concerned. The African sects in Southern Nyasaland are less spectacular than some of those in other parts of the continent; their members do not wear colourful uniforms or become possessed, and few of them have introduced new doctrines or rituals. Nevertheless I hope to show that an analysis of sectarianism in this area sheds some light on the process of rapid social change which is taking place.

In some parts of Africa, African members of Christian missions have left and started new religious groups, which, although originating with a large content of Christian teaching, have subsequently changed their doctrines, often on the death or banishment of the founder, who then becomes an object of worship. The result is a movement away from the main stream of Christian doctrine.[5] Typically such religious groups are initiated by prophets receiving supernatural revelations.

The African sects in Southern Nyasaland, however, have not been started by prophets, and their doctrines, with few exceptions, remain substantially the same as those of the mission churches from which they have originated. Apart from the Ethiopian Church, whose doctrines are described in Chapter V, the teachings of all the sects with which I had contact diverge little from well-established Protestant theological beliefs.

Some explanation is required of the way in which I use the terms 'sect' and 'church' in this book. Yinger, following Troeltsch and others, bases the distinction between church and sect on their relationship with the established secular order, the church tending to accept and support it and the sect not.[6] This distinction is not a valuable one to employ in Southern Nyasaland, or indeed probably in any colonial or mission situation. Missionaries are generally ex-patriates and their relations and attitudes towards the secular Government in their home country may be very different from their attitude towards the Government of the overseas territory. During my fieldwork, for instance, the Church of Scotland strongly opposed many Government policies and was the centre of much political discontent. In its home country, on

---

[5] This is the case, for instance, in the Kimbangist movements in the Lower Congo (see Anderson, 1958) and in the Lumpa Church founded by Alice Lenshina in Northern Rhodesia (see Rotberg, 1961).

[6] Yinger, 1957, pp. 145–6.

INTRODUCTION

the other hand, the Church of Scotland is the 'established Church' and is scarcely regarded as a hotbed of sedition.

I shall use the criterion of scale to differentiate between churches and sects in Southern Nyasaland. Two missions are very much larger than the remainder. In Mlanje District, where I did most of my field-work, the Roman Catholic Church had 206 congregations and the Church of Scotland 127. The next largest was the Watch Tower, with thirty-nine congregations. I refer to the Church of Scotland and the Roman Catholic Church as 'churches' and the remainder of the Christian religious groups, including Watch Tower, operating in the area as 'sects'. Although this may appear a somewhat arbitrary distinction, a number of other factors are associated with the difference in scale. The fact that the churches are larger leads to a more rigidly defined form of church government than is necessary in the smaller sects where government is conducted largely through face-to-face relationships. In Southern Nyasaland African sects have been formed by secession from other sects; sectarianism in this area has not taken place in the churches, although the Church of Scotland, in particular, has been a fruitful source of recruitment to new sects. The churches, too, have generally developed a wider range of secular educational and welfare services: both have hospitals in the Southern Province, and, with Government assistance, they provide almost all the facilities for education beyond Standard Three.

Within the category of sects I make the broad distinction between 'White sects' and 'African sects'. The White sects are distinguished by the presence of White missionaries resident in Nyasaland. The African sects are those which have been started by Africans and have no White representatives in the territory—in a few cases they are linked to other religious organizations outside the Protectorate and receive occasional visits from officials of these organizations, some of whom are Whites. All the African sects, however, are effectively under African control, and in Southern Africa, where Whites have a high social status *qua* Whites, this is crucial. It is with these African sects that this book is primarily concerned—but they can only be understood against the background of the White sects from which they have seceded and of the rapid social changes resulting from White administration of the Protectorate.

Typically sects are formed as a result of a protest against the state of affairs within an existing religious group. In the history of Christianity, however, not all such protests have resulted directly in the

4 SECTARIANISM IN SOUTHERN NYASALAND

development of a new sect. In Uganda, for instance, the Bamalaki, a group of Anglicans who eschewed the use of European-style medicine, remained within the Anglican Church for some years after they had disagreed with Anglican teachings.[7] In some cases those making the protest have formed a group within the existing Church. These groups are distinguished from sects by the fact that they still recognize the authority of the parent body, although possessing an ecclesiastical organization of their own. The formation of such groups is most typical of the Roman Catholic Church in the pre-Reformation period, when such orders as the Benedictines, Franciscans, Dominicans, and Carmelites were founded.[8] In Southern Nyasaland, however, even what appear to be relatively minor protests easily lead to the formation of new sects. In the traditional social organization of this area disputes led to secessions and the formation of new social groups. It will be shown that the traditional values associated with this process have persisted in the African sects.

Most of the African sects in Southern Nyasaland are of what I term the 'simple secessionist type'. These are not formed as a result of protest against the doctrines or ritual of the parent body, but rather as the result of protests against the organization or individuals within it. Differences of doctrine may be introduced into the new sect after its formation, but they are not its *raison d'être*. This type of sect is also found in other parts of Africa—Sundkler shows how the Ethiopian churches of South Africa have been subjected to continual secessions over the question of leadership,[9] and the African Greek Orthodox Church in Uganda described by Welbourn[10] falls into this category.

One African sect in Southern Nyasaland in which I was able to carry out a limited amount of investigation has introduced new doctrines in the area. This is the Ethiopian[11] Church, which has

---

[7] Welbourn, 1961, p. 34.   [8] Wach, 1947, pp. 186–7.
[9] Sundkler, 1961, pp. 161–7.   [10] Welbourn, 1961, Chapter 5.
[11] This is the title given to this sect by its founder, who spent a number of years in South Africa. The term Ethiopian seems first to have been used in this context by the founder of an African sect in Pretoria in 1892, who is reputed to have based the name on the reference in Psalm 68, 'Ethiopia shall soon stretch out her hands unto God', taking this as a promise of the evangelization of Africa as a whole (see Sundkler, pp. cit., p. 39). Sundkler also uses the term to refer to a category of Bantu independent churches which have 'seceded from White Mission Churches chiefly on racial grounds' or those which have subsequently seceded from these (pp. 53–54). This latter is not a particularly meaningful categorization to use in reference to Southern Nyasaland, where I use the term 'Ethiopian' to refer to the sect which knows itself by that name.

INTRODUCTION 5

attempted to combine elements of traditional beliefs and practices with some of those introduced by missionaries. I use the term 'synthetist' to refer to this type of sect.[12]

The description of the African sects in the following chapters relates to these two categories, 'simple secessionist' and 'synthetist'. Although messianic or millenarian sects are frequently found in areas of rapid social change, and despite rumours of a millenarian or messianic nature existing in Southern Nyasaland in 1958–9, sects in which the idea of a rapidly approaching millennium is paramount were not characteristic of the area at that time.

Ecological and social background

My fieldwork was largely confined to two areas of Southern Nyasaland, Mlanje District, where there are twenty-two African sects, and Chapananga's chieftaincy in Chikwawa District, where there are none. My description and analysis of African sects relates therefore to Mlanje District, but a comparison with conditions in Chapananga's chieftaincy helps to distinguish and define some of the factors involved in their formation.

Mlanje District covers an area of 1,512 square miles. It consists of part of the Shire Highlands and is a fairly level plateau lying between 2,000 and 3,000 feet above sea-level, but containing Mlanje Mountain, a massif which rises to almost 10,000 feet. The total population of the district at the time of the last census in 1945 was 209,522—a density of 138 per square mile. The total population of the Southern Province has been estimated to have increased by 29 per cent between 1945 and 1957,[13] and there is no reason to suppose that the increase in Mlanje was less than the average for the province as a whole. The population density of the District is thus high for Central Africa. Settlements are scattered throughout the District, except for the high mountain areas and a few parts where there is a shortage of water. The typical settlement consists of a cluster of from three to ten huts, and such clusters are found every two to three hundred yards in Mlanje. Most parts of the district are accessible by motor vehicle and a number of daily bus services run through it; only for short spells during the wet season, from November to March, do communications by road present any difficulties. With an average altitude of around 3,000 feet, the climate

---

[12] See Smith, 1957.
[13] *Report of the Secretary for African Affairs*, Zomba, 1957.

6 SECTARIANISM IN SOUTHERN NYASALAND

of the district is attractive for Whites, and the Shire Highlands were the focus of intensive missionary activity even before the beginning of the present century.

Chief Chapananga's area presents many contrasts with Mlanje. It lies in the valley of the River Mwanza, a tributary of the Shire which drains Lake Nyasa into the Zambesi. The lower reaches of the river are flat and swampy and settlement tends to be concentrated along the edges of the flood plain. In 1945 the population of Chikwawa District as a whole was 59,664—a density of 31·4 per square mile, i.e. less than a quarter of the density in Mlanje. In Chapananga's area clusters of three to ten huts occur in the habitable areas, but there are also larger aggregations of from 30 to a hundred huts. Communications are poorer than in Mlanje. The chieftaincy was almost entirely inaccessible by motor vehicle during much of the wet season 1958–9.[14] There are no bus services at all in the chieftaincy. The low altitude of the area results in higher temperatures than in the Shire Highlands; it is thus not so attractive to Whites and in 1959 only two missions, the Roman Catholics and the Zambesi Mission,[15] had congregations in the area, and of these only the Roman Catholics had missionaries resident in Chikwawa District.

The population of Southern Nyasaland as a whole is heterogeneous from the point of view of its ethnic origin. In 1945, 21 per cent of the people in Mlanje were aboriginal Nyanja, 6 per cent were Yao— descendants of invaders who entered Nyasaland from the east during the latter half of the nineteenth century—and 71 per cent Nguru[16] immigrants, or their descendants, who had entered Nyasaland from eastern Portuguese East Africa during the present century. Chikwawa District has not been subject to the same amount of immigration; here the aboriginal Nyanja in 1945 comprised 48 per cent of the population, Cikunda immigrants from western Portuguese East Africa 38 per cent, and Nguru 7 per cent. These categories are, however, only important in determining an individual's ethnic origin, they are of little socio-cultural significance at the present time.[17]

---

[14] Later during 1959 a new all-weather road was built in connecting Chapananga's court with the administrative centre at Chikwawa in the Shire Valley.

[15] This was originally known as the Zambesi Industrial Mission and is still frequently referred to as such.

[16] This is a blanket term used to cover a number of linguistically related peoples who have immigrated into Southern Nyasaland and who usually call themselves Lomwe.

[17] See Chapter III, pp. 27–32.

INTRODUCTION

They are not tribes in the sense that they inhabit a single stretch of territory, nor are they political or cultural units. Intermarriage between the categories is very common, and local groups, villages and chieftaincies are heterogeneous in their ethnic origin.

The social organization of Chapananga's area and Mlanje is basically similar. Descent is reckoned matrilineally and marriage is normally permanently uxorilocal except for heads of matrilineages, village headmen and chiefs. Clusters of huts are occupied by a group of sisters under the care of one of their brothers, together with their spouses, married daughters and their spouses and unmarried male children. This localized matrilineage is known as the *mbumba* and its leader as the *mwini mbumba*. Married male members of the matrilineage living uxorilocally elsewhere are, in certain contexts, considered to be members of the *mbumba*.

There are no larger groups based upon kinship. Dispersed nontotemic exogamous clans exist, but their significance is almost entirely confined to the regulation of marriage. The larger aggregations of huts in Chapananga's area often contain members of a number of unrelated matrilineages, and often matrilineages are not localized within these clusters.

There is competition between matrilineal relatives for the position of *mwini mbumba*, but if two cousins are competing for the position the *mbumba* usually splits into two separate halves.

Clusters of huts are grouped into villages and in both Mlanje and Chapananga's area adjacent clusters may be inhabited by matrilineally or patrilaterally related matrilineages or by unrelated ones. A village may most conveniently be defined as the area ruled over by a village headman recognized by the colonial administration. The headman is normally a matrilineal descendent of the head of the first matrilineage to be given permission to settle in the area. Not all the traditional headmen are recognized by the administration, and so many villages contain village sections ruled over by a *nyakwawa* (i.e. a traditional headman unrecognized by the administration). Rather more prestige is attached to the office of village headman than to that of *nyakwawa* and there is consequently competition for 'books'—the symbol of a headman's office.[18]

None of the ethnic groups represented in Mlanje or Chapananga's area have formed a single centralized State within the period of recorded

---

[18] See Mitchell, 1956, pp. 83–91.

8   SECTARIANISM IN SOUTHERN NYASALAND

history—all were ruled over by a number of petty autonomous chiefs. These chiefs were recognized as the heads, or their descendents, of the first matrilineage to enter a particular area or to overcome the existing inhabitants. By the 1933 Native Authority Ordinance many of these chiefs were appointed Native Authorities and courts were established at their headquarters with clerks, tax officials, messengers, and other features of a Western bureaucratic system. The system of petty autonomous chiefs has, however, been preserved under the colonial administration.

Traditionally the political units as well as the matrilineages were subject to fission. Heads of matrilineages who wished to start new villages could do so if they could find sufficient support. Similarly village headmen could move out of the chieftaincy and set themselves up as chiefs in another area if they could find enough other headmen to support them. This is much more difficult today, particularly in Mlanje, where the vast increase in population means that there is little land available for the creation of new political units; moreover, Native Authorities and village headmen in both Mlanje and Chapananga's area are now officials in an administrative hierarchy supported by a Government which is reluctant to disturb it.[19] An appreciation of this change in the political organization, which is described in greater detail in Chapter VII, is fundamental to an understanding of sectarianism in this area, since, as will be shown, African sects provide opportunities for leadership for some of those who now lack them in the political sphere.

Traditionally religious grouping was conterminous with other social groupings in both areas. The traditional religious beliefs centred round the veneration of matrilineal ancestral spirits. The head of the matrilineage was responsible for making offerings, on behalf of the matrilineage, to the spirits of his deceased predecessors. Similarly the chief and village headman were each responsible for making offerings to their predecessors for their chieftaincy or village, the chief having the special responsibility of supplicating his predecessors for rain for the chieftaincy. The belief in a supreme divinity appears to have been indigenous to the areas, but such a belief does not appear to have been the basis for any social action.[20] Thus there were no specifically religious officials; religious authority was vested in those

---

[19] See Mitchell, 1949, and Wishlade, 1961.
[20] Werner, 1906, p. 48.

INTRODUCTION

with kinship and political authority. All the specifically religious groups in both areas are Christian, except for a few Islamic congregations in Mlanje—most of whose members are Yao.[21]

---

[21] The Yao were in contact with Arabs on the east coast of Africa during the nineteenth century and many adopted Islam from them.

S.S.N.–B

II

THE ORIGINS OF THE SECTS

LIVINGSTONE was the first British explorer to enter what is now Southern Nyasaland, and he recorded his descriptions of the country at some length.[1] Although he visited neither Chapananga's area nor what is now Mlanje District, he passed close to both. He first travelled up the Shire river in 1859, and in the same year crossed the 'Mang'anja Highlands' (now known as the Shire Highlands) and discovered Lake Shirwa. He described 'Milanje' Mountain,[2] and passed through an environment essentially similar in topography to Mlanje District.

He described the oppressive heat of the Shire Valley and contrasts this with the more pleasant conditions in the Highlands, suggesting that in the latter 'our countrymen might enjoy good health and also be of signal benefit, by leading the multitude of industrious inhabitants to cultivate cotton, buaze, sugar. . . .'[3] As a result of Livingstone's enthusiasm for the country the first mission station was started in Nyasaland in 1861 at Magomero in what is now Zomba District. Livingstone personally conducted the first missionaries, Bishop Mackenzie and his fellow Anglican representatives of the Universities' Mission to Central Africa, to the Highlands. In 1862 a representative of the Free Church of Scotland, James Stewart, arrived to look round the Shire Highlands for a further site for a mission station.[4] Livingstone remarks on this occasion that the Anglicans would be unlikely to feel any jealousy as there was 'room for hundreds of missions'.[5] Certainly less than a century later more than forty had found room.

The Anglican missionaries were forced to withdraw in 1862 as a result of continual conflict with Yao slave raiders. James Stewart withdrew without establishing a mission. The Universities' Mission to Central Africa returned to Nyasaland in 1881, but this time to Likoma Island in Lake Nyasa, and they have subsequently concentrated their activities in Central Nyasaland and have not established congregations in either Mlanje or Chapananga's area.

Livingstone's favourable description of the Shire Highlands was

---

[1] Livingstone, 1865.   [2] Ibid., p. 82.   [3] Ibid., p. 127.
[4] Ibid., p. 413.   [5] Ibid., p. 414.

THE ORIGINS OF THE SECTS

not, however, forgotten. The first effective mission station to be established in Nyasaland was started in Blantyre in 1876, by Scots missionaries sent out as the result of a joint effort by the established Church of Scotland and the Free Church of Scotland, the former sending missionaries to Blantyre and the latter to Livingstonia at Cape MacLear on the shores of Lake Nyasa.[6]

The foundation of the Church of Scotland mission at Blantyre preceded the British Government's proclamation of a Protectorate in the area round the Shire by some thirteen years. During this period the Scots missionaries found themselves acting as *de facto* political officials as well as missionaries.[7] Blantyre was not an indigenous political centre, but has subsequently become the largest town and commercial centre of Nyasaland.

The Church of Scotland[8] established the first mission station in Mlanje in 1890 on the foothills of the mountain near the present administrative headquarters of the district. Today it has 127 congregations in Mlanje District.

In 1959 twenty-eight independent religious groups were operating in Mlanje District. Of these I had personal contact with twenty-two. Ten of these were missions with White missionaries resident in Nyasaland, and twelve were entirely under African control. Eighteen of the twenty-two are linked historically with the activities of Joseph Booth.[9] The remaining four are the Church of Scotland, the Roman Catholics, the Assemblies of God, and the African Church Crucified Mission.

The Roman Catholics, with 206 congregations, have by far the largest membership in Mlanje. The missionaries in charge are Montfarist Marist fathers, members of a French Order founded in the eighteenth century who established their first mission station in Nyasaland at Mzama near Ncheu in the Central Province in 1901,

---

[6] Livingstonia was later re-sited nearer the northern end of the Lake.

[7] Hanna, 1956, pp. 23–32.

[8] The two branches of the Church of Scotland joined with the Dutch Reformed Church in 1924 to form the Church of Central Africa (Presbyterian). The Dutch Reformed Church has no congregations in either Mlanje or Chapananga's area and is largely confined to the Central Province. Members of the C.C.A.(P.) in the Southern Province still refer to themselves as members of the Church of Scotland, and non-members call themselves 'wa-Scotland'. Only a few higher officials stress that they are members of the C.C.A.(P.). It is in conformity with this general usage that I use the title Church of Scotland for that branch of the C.C.A.(P.) operating in the Southern Province.

[9] See below.

SECTARIANISM IN SOUTHERN NYASALAND

but soon afterwards established stations at Blantyre and other parts of the Shire Highlands and the Shire Valley.

The Assemblies of God is an American mission which established its first Southern African missions in the Union of South Africa. It extended its work to Nyasaland in the 1930's, when a White missionary was sent to establish a mission in the Shire Highlands at Limbe.

My contacts with the African Church Crucified Mission were at the time when a 'state of emergency' was declared in Nyasaland after political upheavals in March 1959, and despite several visits to a congregation of this sect I was unable to obtain any reliable information about its history. It has one congregation in N.A. Nazombe's area of Mlanje District, but its headquarters are in the Ncheu District of the Central Province.

The activities of Joseph Booth have been recounted in detail by Shepperson and Price.[10] They describe Booth as a 'religious hitchhiker'—an apt description for a man who was responsible for introducing no fewer than seven missions into Nyasaland. Six of the missions he introduced now have congregations in Mlanje.

Joseph Booth, an Englishman, emigrated to Australia as a young man. While in Australia he felt himself called to establish an interdenominational and self-propagating 'industrial mission' in Africa. Accordingly in 1892 he came to Africa and examined the prospects for such a mission in several areas in the southern part of the continent. Like Livingstone, he was impressed by the possibilities of development in the Shire Highlands. Originally his aim had been to settle 'at least fifty miles from any mission station', but he was forced by sickness and the failure of his resources to establish the first of his missions, the Zambesi Industrial Mission, in August 1892 at Mitsidi, only some five miles away from the Church of Scotland Mission at Blantyre.[11] This brought him into conflict with the Scots missionaries, who considered he was prosyletizing among their converts. However, the mission became firmly established and a number of outlying congregations were later set up in Mlanje. The Z.I.M. is also one of the two missions operating in Chapananga's area.

---

[10] Their book, *Independent African* (1958), describes the rising led by John Chilembwe in 1915 and the events leading up to it. Chilembwe was Booth's servant, who subsequently founded the Providence Industrial Mission, the first of the completely African sects in Nyasaland. The authors give a detailed history of this and other sects.

[11] Shepperson and Price, op. cit., p. 32.

THE ORIGINS OF THE SECTS

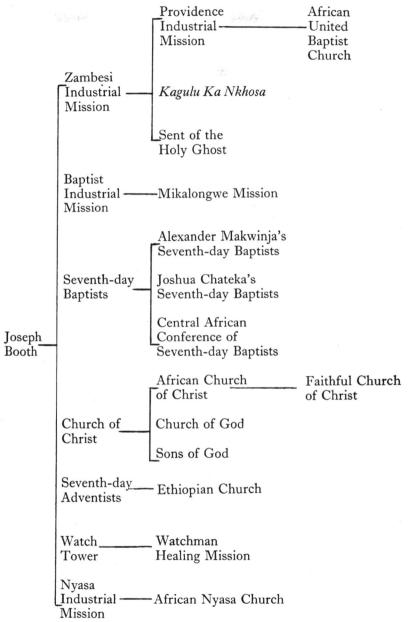

FIG. 1. The historical development of sects in Southern Nyasaland

14 SECTARIANISM IN SOUTHERN NYASALAND

After launching the Z.I.M., Booth turned his attention to establishing another similar mission to be financed from Australia. As a result the Nyasa Industrial Mission was started, in 1893. The site chosen was again in the Shire Highlands, this time in the Likabula valley, a few miles north of Blantyre and not far from the Z.I.M. headquarters at Mitsidi. It was, and still is, completely independent of the Z.I.M., although today they do exchange preachers and the White missionaries co-operate in other ways. The N.I.M. now has seven congregations in Mlanje.

In 1895 Booth made an appeal in Scotland for support for another industrial mission; as a result the Baptist Industrial Mission was established at Gowa, near Ncheu, in what is now the Central Province, about 100 miles north of Blantyre. Soon, however, Booth and the missionary sent out disagreed with each other,[12] and the mission became independent of Booth's control. It was taken over by the Churches of Christ in 1929. Although the Baptist Industrial Mission does not appear to have had congregations in Mlanje, there are now a number of congregations belonging to offshoots from it.

Booth also visited the United States in an attempt to find support for his missionary ventures, and returned in 1899 as the agent of an American group, the Seventh-day Baptists. He bought land for them in the Cholo area of the Shire Highlands some thirty miles south of Blantyre sufficient for a plantation for another mission on the 'industrial' pattern.[13] Again conflicts developed between Booth and the parent body and the latter withdrew its support in 1901. They later sent their own missionary in 1914 to take charge of the station, but this missionary was deported after the 1915 rising,[14] and the mission was entirely under African control for some time. It subsequently split into several independent groups, three of which are still operating in Mlanje; two of these are under African leadership and one under a White missionary.

After breaking with the Seventh-day Baptists, Booth made contact with the Seventh-day Adventists in the United States. An American Negro missionary was sent to Nyasaland to found a mission station, again in the Cholo area of the Shire Highlands; but Booth soon broke with the Seventh-day Adventists and was formally 'dis-fellowshipped' in 1906.[15] The mission continued successfully, however, and soon

---

[12] Shepperson and Price, op. cit., p. 64.
[13] Ibid., p. 134.   [14] Ibid., p. 333.   [15] Ibid., p. 148.

THE ORIGINS OF THE SECTS

White American missionaries were sent. They now have twenty-three congregations in Mlanje.

At some time between 1902 and 1904 Booth was deported from Nyasaland, but even after this he was indirectly responsible for introducing two more religious groups into the country. He went to America again in 1906 and met Russell, the author of the 'Millennial Dawn' pamphlets out of which the Watch Tower movement grew. In 1907, when Booth was in the Union of South Africa, he was visited by one of his former converts, Kamwana. Booth taught him the Watch Tower doctrine and he returned to Nyasaland to preach. He had considerable success in the area inhabited by the Tonga to the west of Lake Nyasa, not far from the Free Church of Scotland's mission headquarters at Livingstonia. Booth maintained his connexions with Watch Tower in Nyasaland for a few years by sending literature to them, and also by meeting Nyasa labour migrants in the Union of South Africa. Watch Tower had no White representatives in Nyasaland until 1925, but it had gained considerable support under African control, and had spread southwards to the Shire Highlands. They now have thirty-nine congregations in Mlanje—the largest number belonging to any religious group except the Church of Scotland and Roman Catholics.

In 1906, Booth was also in contact with the British Churches of Christ, attempting to interest them in missionary work in Central Africa. However, his proposals were rejected on the grounds that he was considered to be too much implicated in politics. He then turned to the South African Churches of Christ, who sent a White missionary who first established himself at Chikunda, an old station of Booth's a few miles north of Blantyre and not far from Mitsidi. Later the headquarters of the Churches of Christ were transferred to another part of the Shire Highlands—to Namiwawa near Zomba. The Churches of Christ now have six congregations in Mlanje.

The first of the entirely African sects in Nyasaland was the Providence Industrial Mission, known at first as the Ajawa (i.e. Yao) Providence Industrial Mission. The development of the sect and the activities of its founder have been described in detail by Shepperson and Price, and the title of their book, *Independent African*, refers to Chilembwe himself. Chilembwe was a servant in Booth's household and became a member of the Zambesi Industrial Mission. In 1897 he accompanied Booth to the United States, where he remained for some two years, receiving theological training in a Negro Baptist seminary.

16   SECTARIANISM IN SOUTHERN NYASALAND

On his return he started the Providence Industrial Mission at Chiradzulu, in the Shire Highlands, some fifteen miles from Blantyre. It aimed at being another self-propagating 'Industrial Mission' on the pattern of those established by Booth. Chilembwe was assisted for a few years by a number of American Negroes, but they left in 1906, leaving him in sole control of the new sect.

Thus by the end of the first decade of the present century no fewer than eight separate religious groups had established congregations in the Shire Highlands. All except two established their first Nyasaland congregations in this area; the remaining two—Watch Tower and the Roman Catholics—started further north, but very soon extended their activities southwards into the Shire Highlands.

In contrast, no missions were founded in the Shire Valley, and only three extended their activities to this area—the Roman Catholics, Church of Scotland, and the Zambesi Industrial Mission. Topographical factors appear to have been at least partly responsible for this difference. Livingstone and the early missionaries, although travelling up the Shire Valley and relying on the river as their link with the outside, made the journey up the escarpment into the Highlands, and once the Church of Scotland Mission had been established at Blantyre it attracted other missions. The advantages of using the lines of communication already pioneered by the Scots missionaries seem to have outweighed the advantages of starting work in 'virgin territory'.

Livingstone pointed out the possibilities of developing cotton-growing in the Shire Valley, and it has certainly become the most important cash crop in the area today. It did not, however, attract the missionaries. Both the Zambesi Industrial Mission and the Roman Catholics established congregations in Chapananga's area before 1910, but since then no other religious groups have established themselves there. Only the Roman Catholics today have White missionaries resident in Chikwawa District. Even today missionaries from the Zambesi Mission consider that the Mwanza Valley has not been a successful area from their point of view. It is still thought to be remote and unhealthy for Whites, and the White missionaries from the Zambesi Mission visit it only occasionally during the dry season. By road the distance between Blantyre and the lower reaches of the Mwanza is rather less than the distance between Blantyre and parts of Mlanje, but as a result apparently of the more favourable climate early missionary activity was concentrated in the Highlands, and this concentration has persisted to the present day. The establishment of many

THE ORIGINS OF THE SECTS

different missions in the Shire Highlands provided the basis, and indeed the example, for further secession and the subsequent formation of African sects. Before these secessions took place, however, the Chilembwe Rising of 1915 focused the attention of the Government and others upon the small missions, which Booth had introduced.

The rising, which was led by John Chilembwe, founder of the P.I.M., took place in the Shire Highlands, where there were attacks on White employees at a plantation at Magomero near Zomba, on the Mandala Trading Company's store at Blantyre, and on the Roman Catholic Mission also at Blantyre. There was a smaller simultaneous rising at Ncheu in the Central Province, where some of the smaller missions introduced by Booth had also been active.[16] The Shire Valley does not seem to have been affected.

As a result of the rising the Providence Industrial Mission was closed down by the Government and many of its members, including Chilembwe, lost their lives. The Government also deported White missionaries of the Seventh-day Baptists and the Churches of Christ on suspicion of having been associated with subversive activities.

The P.I.M. was allowed to start again in 1926 under Dr. Daniel Malekebu, one of its early members—and a Nyasaland African who had gone to the United States in 1906 and so was absent from the country in 1915.

The seven sects started by Booth, together with the P.I.M., may be regarded as the parent generation from which the remaining African sects in the Shire Highlands have seceded. My information on these African sects has been derived from interviews with the leaders or other officials of the sects concerned, and by attendance at their meetings and services and discussions with their members and their neighbours. The origin of these sects is illustrated diagrammatically in Fig. 1.

In the Seventh-day Baptist Church and the Churches of Christ the expulsion of the White missionaries indirectly led to secessions. The Seventh-day Baptists virtually collapsed under Government pressure after 1915. Two of the missionary's African assistants, Alexander Makwinja and Joshua Chateka, were imprisoned for alleged complicity in the rising. When they were released in the mid 1920's they each formed separate sects, both taking the name Seventh-day Baptists. Members of Chateka's sect told me that Makwinja was released

---

[16] For a full account of the rising, see Shepperson and Price, 1958, Chapter VI.

18   SECTARIANISM IN SOUTHERN NYASALAND

first and introduced new rules forbidding members to wear cloths on their heads and enjoining them to wear beads round their necks. When Chateka was released he disagreed with these new rules and started an independent sect in the Central Province. Both sects now have branches in Mlanje, in some cases they have congregations in adjacent villages, and both have contacts with the Seventh-day Baptists in the United States, though neither receives financial support from there. Makwinja was in charge of his sect in 1958–9. Chateka was also still recognized as head of his sect in spite of being detained in Zomba Mental Hospital at that time. Eventually White Seventh-day Baptist missionaries were allowed to return to the Protectorate, and an Australian missionary established a mission at Sandama in the Cholo District, near to the Portuguese East African border. This sect, known as the Central African Conference of Seventh-day Baptists, now has six congregations in Mlanje and appears to have drawn some of its support from former members of Makwinja's and Chateka's sects.

When the Churches of Christ missionaries were deported in 1915 the sect continued under African leadership until 1929, when another White missionary arrived to take over. The missionary soon quarrelled with an African minister, Masangano, over the question of the baptism of people expelled from the Church of Scotland. Masangano then left and founded a new sect, the Church of God. At the same time the African Church of Christ was founded by another African minister in the Church of Christ. Later two other sects, the Church of Christ in Africa and the Sons of God, seceded from the Church of Christ.

In 1950 an American missionary from an American Church of Christ in Los Angeles visited the African Churches of Christ with the object of giving it financial support. He was, however, dissatisfied with the organization of this sect and encouraged E. C. Severe, a teacher in the African Church of Christ, to form a new sect, the Faithful Church of Christ. This receives financial support from the United States, but is entirely under African control, apart from visits from American members of the Church of Christ which have taken place every four years or so since its foundation. The headquarters of the Faithful Church of Christ are in Mlanje District. It is with the Faithful Church of Christ that I have had most contact, living at its headquarters for some three months.

There have been numerous attempts at further secession from the various Churches of Christ, including three attempts at secession from

THE ORIGINS OF THE SECTS

the Faithful Church of Christ. None of them has, however, succeeded in establishing a regular congregation with a church building or prayer house in Mlanje.

The expulsion of White missionaries in 1915 was not, however, the only factor leading to secession, and probably not the crucial factor. Secessions also took place from those missions retaining their White missionaries.

There are two sects with congregations in Mlanje whose founders were previously members of the Zambesi Industrial Mission. The founder of the Sent of the Holy Ghost Church, Maloya, was previously a minister in the Zambesi Mission. He told me that in 1927, a White missionary introduced a law into the sect forbidding smoking and the consumption of sweet beer. He suggested that the introduction of these laws led to quarrelling and that there was no righteousness in the mission. Maloya therefore left and founded a sect of his own, the Sent of the Holy Ghost Church, whose members were initially largely drawn from the Zambesi Mission. This new sect was composed of members who kept these new rules, he said. The quarrel was not with the rules themselves but with the fact that the members of the mission were not keeping them. In 1956 Maloya met with a White American missionary from the Pentecostal Holiness Church, who was working in Lusaka in Northern Rhodesia. As a result of this meeting the Sent of the Holy Ghost Church became part of the Pentecostal Holiness Mission. Maloya stated that he found that the teachings of the two sects were the same, so he was being sent financial help from America and had taken the name Pentecostal Holiness Church for his sect. The White missionary from Lusaka now visits him annually, but Maloya is still in full control in Nyasaland. The affiliation with the American sect led to a split in the Sent of the Holy Ghost Church, the second-in-command attempting to form a new sect of his own. (Maloya suggested that he was doing this as he was jealous of the money that he himself was now receiving.) The second-in-command has not yet succeeded in establishing a regular congregation with its own church building. The Pentecostal Holiness Church now has one congregation in Mlanje, while its headquarters are in the adjacent district of Chiradzulu.

The founder of the *Kagulu ka Nkhosa* (the Congregation of the Lamb), the Reverend Rogers, was an elder in the Zambesi Industrial Mission who also stated that he left and founded a sect of his own because the members of the Zambesi Mission were not adhering to

20 SECTARIANISM IN SOUTHERN NYASALAND

its rules. This sect was founded in 1932 in Mlanje District, but still has only one congregation and receives no financial support beyond the contributions of its members. Rogers states that two former members of the *Kagulu ka Nkhosa* have left and attempted to form sects of their own, but have met with little success.

There has been one successful secession from the Nyasa Industrial Mission—the African Nyasa Mission was started in 1946 by Phombeya, a former pastor in the Nyasa Industrial Mission. The African Nyasa Mission has no congregations in Mlanje, but its headquarters and three other congregations are in the adjacent Cholo District. Phombeya stated that while he was a pastor in the N.I.M. he was accused of witchcraft by his wife's brother, a teacher at the school attached to his congregation. Most of the congregation apparently supported the teacher and so the case was taken to the Native Authority, but was not proved. Phombeya therefore decided to leave the N.I.M. and start a sect of his own. He has been more successful than Maloya or Rogers, having several congregations and a Government-supported school attached to his sect. He also stated that the relations between himself and the Industrial Mission are now good.

The African United Baptist Church was started in 1946 by a former pastor in the Providence Industrial Mission, Nakule. Nakule had a disagreement with Dr. Malekebu, the head of the P.I.M., and affiliated his new sect with another of the same name with its headquarters in Johannesburg. Both the Providence Industrial Mission and the African United Baptist Church are associated with the same Negro Baptist group in the United States. It has its headquarters in the Zomba District adjacent to Mlanje and has eleven congregations in Mlanje.

The Ethiopian Church, popularly known as the *Calici ca Makolo* (the Church of the Ancestors), was founded by Peter Nyambo in the Ncheu District of the Central Province. Nyambo was a member of the Seventh-day Adventists in 1910, but in 1914 went to London with a petition for the King complaining about conditions in Nyasaland. He returned to South Africa, but did not return to Nyasaland until some twenty-seven years later.[17] He founded the Ethiopian Church shortly after his return from South Africa. At the end of 1958 there were ten congregations in Mlanje, but it expanded rapidly during the following year, a phenomenon which was associated with political

---

[17] Shepperson and Price, op. cit., pp. 203–9.

THE ORIGINS OF THE SECTS

upheaval in the Protectorate and which is discussed in Chapter VII.

The process of sectarianism in the Shire Highlands has not been confined to the formation of entirely African sects. The Mikalongwe Mission was started in 1929 at Mikalongwe in the Cholo District by Cuthbert Smith, a White missionary sent out from the United Kingdom to the Baptist Industrial Mission. He had a disagreement with the missionary in charge and so left and founded a sect of his own. The Mikalongwe Mission has ten congregations in Mlanje.

In this chapter I have attempted to indicate the origins of the successful sects operating in Mlanje. For every founder of a sect who has succeeded in establishing and maintaining congregations several have attempted and failed. In later chapters I shall attempt to show the processes and forces resulting in the formation of these new African sects and congregations.

III

THE INCIDENCE AND EXTENT OF SECTARIANISM IN SOUTHERN NYASALAND

IN this chapter I attempt to describe the incidence and extent of sectarianism in relation to geographical and cultural factors, and to assess quantitatively the importance of the African sects in relation to the total Christian population.

Table I shows the proportions of people calling themselves Christians or pagans in the censuses which I made of a few villages in the Shire Highlands and in Chapananga's area. Unfortunately my quantitative data relate only to a very small sample indeed, for the figures are based upon a count of only 247 adults; this was largely due to the difficulty of carrying out village censuses during the political upheavals of 1958–9. Moreover, particularly in the case of the Shire Highlands, they may be atypical of the total population, since, in some cases, my entrée into particular villages was through an African sect. This means that the figure of 68 per cent shown in the table as the proportion of Christians of all churches and sects in the Shire Highlands may well be rather higher than the true figure for the whole population.

A further complication arises when one attempts to define the term 'Christian' in this context. For the present purposes I have applied the term 'Christian' to all those who stated that they were so. Clearly the basis of membership of a congregation varies from one religious group to another. In the sects baptism is the generally accepted criterion of membership, though some people not baptized but attending services may consider themselves members.

To put sectarianism in Mlanje in perspective some quantitative assessment of the proportion of Christians belonging to the various churches and sects in the district is necessary. This is difficult to estimate with any degree of accuracy; not only does the basis of membership vary from one religious group to another, but there is also a great deal of variation in the reliability of the membership figures given by the officials of the various churches and sects. Figures for church attendance given by the Faithful Church of Christ, for instance, were approximately three times the actual numbers which I recorded.

THE INCIDENCE AND EXTENT OF SECTARIANISM 23

Table I

NUMBERS OF PAGANS AND CHRISTIANS AS OBTAINED FROM FIELD CENSUSES

Mlanje District:

	Pagans				Christians		
	M	F	Total		M	F	Total
	25	18	43		35	57	92

Chapananga's Area:

	Pagans				Christians		
	M	F	Total		M	F	Total
	31	35	66		19	27	46
			109				138
					Grand Total		247

PERCENTAGES

	Pagans				Christians		
	M	F	Total		M	F	Total
	%	%	%		%	%	%
Mlanje District	42	25	32		58	75	68
Chapananga's Area	62	56	59		38	44	41

It is possible, however, to compare the number of congregations belonging to each religious association in Mlanje. As the permission of the Administration must be obtained before a prayer house or church building can be erected, the Administration's Register of Prayer Houses shows the number of established congregations.[1]

Table II shows a list of congregations in Mlanje in 1959. Out of a total of 576 the Roman Catholic Church and the Church of Scotland have 206 and 127 congregations respectively. Together this represents 57·8 per cent of the total, and thus these two religious groups are of a very different scale from the remaining twenty-six, who possess only 243 congregations between them. The difference in scale is associated with other differences in organization and these will be described in later chapters.

---

[1] It is not generally considered that a congregation has been formed or that officials are truly officials until a building has been erected, see below, p. 122.

Table II

THE DISTRIBUTION OF CONGREGATIONS IN MLANJE

Churches	No. of Congregations	Totals
Roman Catholic	206	
Church of Scotland	127	333
White sects		
Watch Tower	39	
Seventh-day Adventist	23	
Zambesi Industrial Mission	16	
Mikalongwe Mission	10	
Nyasa Industrial Mission	7	
Church of Christ	6	
Central African Conference of Seventh-day Baptists	6	
Assemblies of God	2	
Apostolic Faith Mission	1	110
African sects		
Providence Industrial Mission	28	
Faithful Church of Christ	19	
Seventh-day Baptist (Alexander Makwinja)	14	
Seventh-day Baptist (Joshua Chateka)	12	
Sons of God	12	
African United Baptist Church	11	
Ethiopian Church	10	
African Church of Christ	8	
African Full Gospel Church	5	
Zion Restoration Church	3	
Church of God	3	
Watchman Healing Mission	2	
African Methodist Episcopal Church	2	
African Church Crucified Mission	1	
Mthenga wa Mulungu	1	
Kagulu ka Nkhosa	1	
Sent of the Holy Ghost	1	133
Grand Total		576

THE INCIDENCE AND EXTENT OF SECTARIANISM   25

There are 110 congregations belonging to the nine sects with White missionaries resident in Nyasaland ('White sects'), that is, 19·2 per cent of the total; 133 congregations, or 23 per cent of the total, belong to African sects. The average number of congregations per White sect—12·2 per cent—is higher than the average of 8 per cent for the African sects. These figures do not, of course, give any idea of the total size of the groups of each type, but only of their comparative influence in Mlanje.

The size of congregations varies considerably and visits to a congregation do not always give an accurate picture of its membership. Many African sect officials dislike surprise visits, considering it impolite, and prefer to be warned well in advance of a White visitor. Preparations are then made and this generally results in a larger attendance than normal at the services. Prolonged contact with a single congregation results in a decrease in the attendance at its services as the novelty of having a White visitor in their midst wears off. Visits to several congregations of the same sect in one area also reveal that members of one congregation may attend the services of another if they have heard that a White visitor is likely to be there. Generally, however, the congregations of the Church of Scotland and the Roman Catholic Church are larger than the rest and 200 or more people may attend the services on a Sunday. The congregations of some White sects are also large, though these vary considerably between sects. The congregations of the African sects are usually smaller than those of the White sects, though there are some exceptions to this; the Faithful Church of Christ and the Providence Industrial Mission, for instance, have several congregations where the average attendance at Sunday services is fifty or more. These two are the larger and most successful of the African sects. In some smaller ones, such as the *Kaguluka Nkhosa* and the African Church Crucified Mission, the weekly services may be attended by only about a dozen people.

In general it appears that the size of the congregation corresponds roughly with the total number of congregations in the district. Thus, although 23 per cent of the congregations in Mlanje belong to African sects, the proportion of Christians belonging to these sects is considerably less than this.

In Chapananga's area the proportion of Christians in the total population is smaller. In one village with 112 adult inhabitants forty-six of them, (41 per cent) considered themselves to be Christians.

In this area villages are generally associated with one or other of the

26 SECTARIANISM IN SOUTHERN NYASALAND

two missions operating in the area, the Roman Catholics and the Zambesi Industrial Mission. Informants would say that one village is a 'Catholic Village' while another is a 'Zambesi Mission Village'. This does not mean that all the inhabitants of that village are members of one religious association, but that all, or almost all, the Christians in any village belong to the same congregation. Forty of the forty-six Christians in Tombondera are members of the Zambesi Mission, which has both a school and a prayer house in the village. The remaining six are Roman Catholics: these six consist of the storekeeper and his wife, who have recently moved into the village as employees of the store-owner, two men who have married pagan wives uxorilocally in the village, and one man whose wife also became a Catholic when they married uxorilocally. This situation appears, from observation and discussion with inhabitants of other villages, to be typical of Chapananga's area as a whole. Here the religious affiliation of Christians is largely determined by the denomination of the nearest prayer house.

In Mlanje, on the other hand, there is no such simple correlation, many villages contain two or three prayer houses each belonging to a different religious group. In this area villages, and indeed matri-lineages, are heterogeneous in their religious affiliation.[2] In Mbeza village in N. A. Nazombe's chieftaincy in Mlanje, for example, of the headman's thirty-five adult matrilineal relatives and their spouses resident in the village, sixteen are pagan, nine are members of Watch Tower, three are members of the Church of Scotland, five are Seventh-day Baptists, three are members of the Providence Industrial Mission, and one is a member of the Ethiopian Church. In this area the various religious denominations compete with each other for supporters. Here the density of population is several times greater than that in Chapananga's area, and the pattern of settlement also differs. The pattern of settlement in Mlanje typically consists of a cluster of between three and ten huts, and such clusters are to be found every two or three hundred yards; in the dry season when there is no high maize or other crops to impede the view rarely is one out of sight of such a cluster. In Chapananga's area, on the other hand, most of the population lives in larger settlements, which, however, may be separated from one another by a mile or more of gardens and bush. A prayer house in Mlanje has a much larger potential popula-

---

[2] Bettison reports a similar situation in the peri-urban area of Blantyre/Limbe. (Bettison, 1958, p. 50.)

THE INCIDENCE AND EXTENT OF SECTARIANISM 27

tion from which to recruit its congregation. A corollary of this is that people in Mlanje may have a choice of several prayer houses within easy walking distance of their homes, and may easily change their religious affiliation without a change of residence. In Mlanje an aspiring African pastor is thus likely to find some support if he wishes to found a congregation. In Chapananga's area the distance which people would have to travel limits the size of a potential congregation.

Tribalism

In the Union of South Africa a feature of sectarianism has been the emergence of tribal sects. Tribal loyalties and sentiments have led to the formation of such sects as the Zulu Congregational Church and the Swazi Church of God in Zion.[3] There is no parallel to this situation in Southern Nyasaland. Tribal affiliation in this area is of little significance as a basis for social action. Individuals recognize that they belong to a *mtundu*, a term which is generally translated as 'tribe', and the population is classified into tribes in the Population Census Reports, though this classification has limited significance today.

The aboriginal inhabitants of both Mlanje and Chapananga's area are the Nyanja, who, together with the Cewa and Cipeta farther north, recognize that they are of Maravi stock. They appear to have had a fairly uniform culture and to have spoken a single language, Chi-Nyanja. Before the immigration of Yao, which started around the middle of the nineteenth century, the Nyanja people seem to have occupied almost all Southern Nyasaland. Livingstone in 1860 recorded a myth that the people in this area were at one time 'united under the government of their great chief Undi whose empire extended from Lake Shirwa to the River Loangwa, but after his death it fell to pieces'.[4] It is, however, highly debatable whether or not such a large political unit existed in the area. Throughout the period of recorded history the Nyanja have consisted of a number of petty autonomous chiefdoms. Thus the Nyanja were not organized into a politically centralized State like the Swazi and Zulu, they were a cultural and linguistic unit rather than a political one.

The Yao entered Nyasaland at the southern end of Lake Nyasa, coming from that part of Portuguese East Africa to the east of the Lake and between the Rovuma and Lujenda rivers.[5] They started moving into Nyasaland around the middle of the nineteenth century

---

[3] See Sundkler, 1961, p. 323. [4] Livingstone, 1865, p. 128. [5] Mitchell, 1956, p. 22.

28   SECTARIANISM IN SOUTHERN NYASALAND

and a considerable number had settled in the Shire Highlands when the Church of Scotland missionaries established themselves at Blantyre in 1876[6] This was not a co-ordinated military invasion but rather a movement of matrilineally linked family groups similar in composition to those of the Nyanja. Some settled peacefully among the aboriginal Nyanja, but more frequently they either set themselves up as rulers over them or pushed them into more remote parts of the country. In Mlanje in 1945 6 per cent of the population were Yao, but three of the six chiefs recognized by the Government were Yao chiefs. The invading Yao were slave raiders and took slaves to trade with the Arabs on the east coast. The Yao immigration did not penetrate to the Shire Valley.

The Yao, too, were not a single political unit, they were also organized into a number of petty autonomous chiefdoms. They appear to have been culturally similar to the Nyanja, speaking a language related to, but not mutually intelligible with, Chi-Nyanja. The main cultural distinctions seem to have been in their different initiation ceremonial and the adherence of some Yao to Islam.

The Yao have not been the only people to immigrate into Nyasaland from Portuguese East Africa. A striking feature of the history of the territory since the establishment of the British Protectorate in 1893 has been the large and prolonged immigration of Nguru people into the Shire Highlands and Chikunda people into the Lower Shire Valley. The Nguru, who call themselves Lomwe, had become the second largest 'tribe' in the 1945 Population Census Report. Numerically they dominate much of the Shire Highlands and in Mlanje they represented 71 per cent of the total population in 1945. These immigrants have come in small matrilineally linked family groups and, in some instances, have attached themselves to existing Yao and Nyanja headmen, and in others established new villages of their own. The domestic and political organization of these immigrants appears to have been similar to that of the Nyanja and Yao, but they were originally linguistically distinct and had their own distinctive initiation ceremonial. They were not linguistically homogeneous; the terms Nguru and Lomwe are blanket terms applied to a number of linguistic groups which have come from that part of Portuguese East Africa which lies to the east of Nyasaland and south of the traditional home of the Yao.

---

[6] MacDonald, 1882, Part 1, p. 31.

THE INCIDENCE AND EXTENT OF SECTARIANISM 29

Immigration from the west, from that part of Portuguese East Africa between Nyasaland and the Zambesi, has been on a smaller scale. Nevertheless there has been a considerable influx of Chikunda people into the Lower Shire Valley, and in 1945 Chikunda and Sena immigrants comprised 40 per cent of the population of Chikwawa District. These immigrants, like the Nguru, have either attached themselves to existing Nyanja headmen or been given land by chiefs to start new villages of their own.

Today, therefore, the population of Mlanje is made up of aboriginal Nyanja, invading Yao, and immigrant Nguru, while Chapananga's area is populated by Nyanja and immigrant Chikunda. The immigration of people from Portuguese East Africa has not created a rigid ethnic hierarchy. The traditional organization of the immigrants appears to have been similar to that of the Nyanja and they have been absorbed into each others' villlages and chieftaincies. Intermarriage between members of different 'tribes' is frequent, and 'tribal' affiliation does not appear to be a significant factor in the choice of a spouse. In both areas village headmen of all 'tribes' are to be found and the composition of villages is heterogeneous in its tribal origins. Immigrant Nguru headmen, for instance, may have Nyanja subjects and vice versa. 'Tribal' affiliation is acquired matrilineally, and so matrilineages are tribally homogeneous, but social groups containing members of more than one matrilineage may be heterogeneous in their 'tribal' affiliation.

As far as the distribution of political offices is concerned, the proportion of village headmen belonging to each 'tribe' is roughly similar to the 'tribal' distribution of the total population as a whole, in both Mlanje and Chapananga's area. At the level of the chiefs or Native Authorities, however, the Nyanja and Yao predominate. Chapananga is Nyanja (as indeed are all the Native Authorities in Chikwawa District); in Mlanje three Native Authorities are Nyanja and three are Yao. The Government in appointing Native Authorities recognized the indigenous 'principle of primacy', whereby the chief was the head of the first matrilineage to enter a particular area and establish control over it; thus no immigrant chiefs have been appointed Native Authorities.[7]

Whatever cultural differences traditionally existed between the various 'tribes' have now largely disappeared. The Nyanja language is

---

[7] See Wishlade, 1961, pp. 36–45.

30 SECTARIANISM IN SOUTHERN NYASALAND

the *lingua franca* in Mlanje and Chapananga's area and throughout almost all southern Nyasaland.[8] Nyanja has been adopted by the Administration as the official vernacular, is used for teaching in schools, for worship in all the churches and sects, and is the language into which the Bible and hymnbooks have been translated. In the tribally heterogeneous Copperbelt of Northern Rhodesia differences of languages have been significant in encouraging the development of at least one sect; here the African Methodist Episcopal Church at Nchanga has received much support from Ndebele Christians because the local pastor is an Ndebele-speaker.[9] This has not occurred in Southern Nyasaland, where Nguru and Chikunda habitually use the Nyanja language in their daily lives and where in many cases descendants of immigrants know no other African language.

Other cultural differences between the inhabitants of the Shire Highlands and Chapananga's area have also largely disappeared. Traditionally there appear to have been differences in their initiation ceremonial; the Nyanja, for instance, did not initiate boys.[10] Today only a small proportion of adolescents are initiated, and members of different *mitundu* may be initiated together either by immigrant or by Nyanja headmen.

Tribal origins are thus not significant for socio-cultural units in this part of Nyasaland. Africans here are more conscious of their identity as Africans and as Nyasalanders than as members of a particular tribe. In the formation of social groups and as a factor in interpersonal relations, the division of the population into Africans, Asians, and Whites is more significant than tribal divisions. Informants refer to themselves as 'Ife Africans' (we Africans) or 'Ife anthu akuda' (we Black people) rather than as Nyanja or Yao.

Tribalism is not associated with the development of African political parties in Nyasaland. The Malawi Party, which is by far the most important political party in the territory, draws its support from members of all 'tribes'.

When Chilembwe first started the Providence Industrial Mission in 1900 it was known as the 'Ajawa (i.e. Yao) Providence Industrial Mission.[11], but the tribal designation seems to have been dropped

---

[8] Atkins estimated in 1949 that only 4 per cent of the population of Mlanje and three per cent of the population of Chikawa and Port Herald (i.e. the Lower Shire Valley) were unable to speak Nyanja. (Atkins, 1950, p. 36.)

[9] Taylor and Lehmann, 1961, p. 220.

[10] Werner, 1906, p. 127.

[11] Shepperson and Price, 1958, p. 127.

THE INCIDENCE AND EXTENT OF SECTARIANISM   31

shortly after its foundation and certainly today this sect contains many more Nguru members than Yao.

Some informants, particularly Nyanja, suggest that the immigrants in Mlanje preferred the African and other small sects, while the Nyanja and Yao preferred the Roman Catholic Church and the Church of Scotland. I found no evidence in any of my village censuses to support this. Apart from the fact that the majority of Moslems (though not all) are Yao, there appears to be no significant correlation between religious affiliation and 'tribal' affiliation. Bettison found a similar situation in the peri-urban area of Blantyre/Limbe. Commenting on a table showing the religious affiliation and 'tribal' origin of the inhabitants of seventeen villages in this area he states: 'Thus the only conclusion that can be drawn is that the Yao tend to adhere somewhat more to the Church of Scotland and the Ngoni to the Roman Catholic Church than to any other denomination'.[12] The incidence of sectarianism in Southern Nyasaland is therefore not limited by tribal factors.

In Southern Nyasaland African sects appear to be restricted to the rural area. They seem to be absent from the towns of Blantyre/Limbe.[13] In contrast to the Union of South Africa sectarianism in Southern Nyasaland is a rural rather than an urban phenomenon.[14]

There are a number of possible explanations for this difference. African sect leaders themselves, when asked why they had not expanded their activities into the town where there was a concentration of people from which they could recruit a potential congregation, stated that the cost of erecting a church building there was too high, and that permission had to be obtained from the administration before it could be built.[15] In the rural areas the permission of the village headman and the chief are all that is required and it is much cheaper to erect a prayer house in a rural village. Sundkler points out

---

[12] Bettison, 1958, p. 51.

[13] I have not carried out fieldwork myself in the town, but Dr. Bettison and a team of African social research assistants from the Rhodes-Livingstone Institute carried out a project from 1958–60 and none of the research assistants found any African sects.

[14] Among the Tswana of the Taung Rserve, Pauw found that the headquarters of the African sects in the reserves were in the towns of the Witwatersrand, while the older missions mostly originated in the rural areas and spread into the towns. (Pauw, 1960, p. 105.)

[15] Under the Town and Country Planning Ordinance No. 30, 1948, the Blantyre/Limbe Town Planning Committee has to approve the plans for the erection of prayer houses in the urban area.

32 SECTARIANISM IN SOUTHERN NYASALAND

how on the Rand many urban congregations of African sects are subsidized by their rural counterparts.[16] Taylor and Lehmann also state that in the Northern Rhodesian Copperbelt town of Chingola, although there are congregations of African sects, only one has been able to erect a church building.[17] Sect leaders are anxious to erect as many prayer houses as possible as an indication of the importance of their sects, but the general economic level of rural Nyasaland is not high enough to support church building in the urban area.

The different types of urban development in Nyasaland and the Rand are also important in this context. Blantyre/Limbe is a commercial rather than an industrial centre, and its location is largely the result of the foundation of the Church of Scotland Mission there in 1876. Johannesburg and the other towns on the Witwatersrand, on the other hand, are industrial centres and their location is the result of the availability of mineral resources. In South Africa the missions were generally established in rural areas and only later moved into towns. There was a great influx of migrant labour into the town and some of these labourers were already Christians and members of mission churches which were unrepresented there. Africans here created their own churches, often to cater for the Christian immigrants unable to find a congregation of their own denomination. In Blantyre/Limbe the missions came first and the towns grew up around them, and there were not large numbers of unattached Christians to provide congregations for African sects.

The urban area of Blantyre/Limbe is obviously much smaller in extent than the large industrial areas of the Witwatersrand and the Rhodesias. Blantyre/Limbe township moreover, lies in a much more densely populated rural area than these industrial centres, and instead of there being large-scale labour migration there is a considerable amount of daily commuting between the town and the surrounding country.[18] Although there are no African sects in the township, it is thus possible that some of those working in the town are members of such sects in the surrounding rural areas of the Shire Highlands. In particular sectarian developments have been particularly marked in the Chiradzulu area near Blantyre, where John Chilembwe established the headquarters of his Providence Industrial Mission. Mlanje District is too far away from Blantyre/Limbe for workers there to be regular members of congregations in this district.

---

[16] Sundkler, 1961, p. 83.   [17] Taylor and Lehmann, 1961, p. 214.
[18] Bettison, op. cit., pp. 24–39.

THE INCIDENCE AND EXTENT OF SECTARIANISM 33

The external connexions of the sects

So far the distinction has been drawn between White sects with White missionaries resident in Nyasaland and African sects without such missionaries. This, however, obscures differences in the nature and extent of the external relations of the sects. We may distinguish between (1) those which are merely a part of an external church organization, (2) those which are of overseas origin but have at least some sort of autonomy in Nyasaland, (3) those of African origin with established external connexions, the most important of which is generally foreign financial support, and, (4) those of African origin which lack any external connexions.

Clearly the Roman Catholic Church falls into the first category, as do some of the White sects such as the Seventh-day Adventists and the Assemblies of God. In the process of 'Africanization' the tendency in some religious groups has been to change from the first to the second category. The Church of Scotland in becoming the Church of Central Africa (Presbyterian) has done this. Some missions were founded with this type of structure; the Zambesi Industrial Mission and the Nyasa Industrial Mission fall into this category.

The most successful of the sects of African origin, in terms of the size of their following, are those with some external connexions and in particular those with financial support. The Providence Industrial Mission and the Faithful Church of Christ are in this category. The Faithful Church of Christ was founded partly on the initiative of an American missionary who came to visit the entirely independent African Church of Christ. It receives money and gifts of clothes and literature from one of the Churches of Christ in Los Angeles. The leader of this sect has also spent several months in the United States, and sends reports of the progress of his sect there. Dr. Malekebu, the leader of the Providence Industrial Mission, also visits and receives money from the National Baptist Convention, the main United States Negro Baptist organization. Nevertheless these are sects which were founded by Africans in Nyasaland and in which Africans have the responsibility for their day-to-day running.

The two African Seventh-day Baptist sects also maintain contact with Seventh-day Baptists in America, exchanging letters with them and also receiving some literature from there. They do not, however, receive American financial support.

The Ethiopian Church is completely independent. Its leader, Peter

34   SECTARIANISM IN SOUTHERN NYASALAND

Nyambo, however, spent some twenty-seven years out of Nyasaland, mostly in the Union of South Africa, and this sect, which differs substantially in its beliefs and practices from the other African sects in Mlanje, exhibits similarities to the Ethiopian type of African sect in South Africa described by Sundkler.[19]

The Sons of God, the African Church of Christ, the Church of God and the *Kagulu ka Nkhosa* have no links outside the Protectorate. They are entirely independent sects, seceding from White sects, but severing their connexions entirely.

Some sects which have no connexions outside Nyasaland have attempted to become associated with sects in the United States. The Sent of the Holy Ghost Church was successful; others have not been so. One official of the Faithful Church of Christ attempted to secede and found a new sect of his own and subsequently to affiliate his congregation with the Church of the Nazarene, an American sect which has recently established a new mission near Limbe. He was unsuccessful. Sect officials are aware that there are a large number of sects in the United States willing to assist in the work of converting Nyasalanders to Christianity. On several occasions I was given a warm welcome by officials of African sects on the assumption that I was an American interested in the sect and looking for a possible extension of missionary activity. Disillusionment led to a rapid deterioration in the degree of *rapport* between us. This desire for affiliation with the United States is partly for financial reasons—some sects receive stipends for their ministers from there—and partly because officials in those sects which are known to be associated with Whites carry a greater prestige than officials in sects which are not. This is a theme which will be discussed in more detail in Chapter VII.

---

[19] Sundkler, op. cit., pp. 38–43.

IV

DOCTRINES OF THE SECTS

The White and simple secessionist sects

FROM the doctrinal point of view there is a basic distinction between the Roman Catholic Church and all the other religious associations in the area. While distinctions do exist between the various Protestant groups, there is a great deal of common ground between them. A theological analysis of the differences between Catholicism and the various Protestant doctrines held in the area is inappropriate here: I merely wish to indicate two basic differences which are significant for a sociological analysis of sectarianism.

The Protestant churches and sects in Mlanje lay greater emphasis upon the Bible and its teachings than do the Catholics, who are more concerned with the teachings of the Church itself. In all the Protestant groups many members have their own copy of the Nyanja translation of the Bible and are encouraged to read and interpret it. Varying interpretations of the Bible provide the doctrinal charter for sectarianism, though in the case of the African sects in Mlanje they are not, as I hope to show, the cause of secession.

A fundamental doctrinal difference between Catholics and Protestants, important to the sociology of sectarianism, is the Catholic doctrine of 'Apostolic Succession' by the 'laying on of hands'. This doctrine postulates that there has been an unbroken historical devolution of authority from Christ through bishops to every properly ordained Catholic priest, and that a priest receives such authority by grace imparted through the ritual of the 'laying on of hands' by a bishop. Such a belief results in an authority structure very different from that of the other religious bodies in Mlanje. Catholic priests possess institutionalized charismatic authority; no other ecclesiastical officials in Mlanje, with whom I had contact, possessed this.[1] The evidence from Mlanje, and from other parts of Africa, suggests that belief in the doctrine of Apostolic Succession, and the consequent possession by priests of institutionalized charisma,

---

[1] I had no contact with the African Methodist Episcopal Church, which holds a similar doctrine. The Anglican Church, which also has its own line of Apostolic Succession, has no congregations in Mlanje.

36   SECTARIANISM IN SOUTHERN NYASALAND

discourages, though it does not prevent, sectarian developments.[2]

Between the various White sects there are many, seemingly minor, differences in doctrine, but doctrinal differences do not appear to be an important factor in the development of African sects. All the sects, both White and African, practise baptism by total immersion and are thus distinguished from both the Church of Scotland and the Roman Catholic Church, which recognize the efficacy of baptism by a token sprinkling. Some sects demand an examination to ensure that those about to be baptized have an elementary knowledge of the fundamentals of the Christian faith, others do not. Most prominent among the latter group are the Churches of Christ, who hold the doctrine of 'Believer's Baptism', whereby all those who declare their belief in Christ are eligible for baptism and thus for membership of the sect.

The teachings of the two original Industrial Missions, introduced by Booth, the Zambesi Mission and the Nyasa Mission, appear very similar and derived essentially from orthodox Baptist teaching. It is the source of their financial support which differentiates them. There is also an interchange of preachers between these two missions, a practice which does not regularly occur in other sects.

The Assemblies of God lay more emphasis upon the power of prayer in the healing of disease than do other sects, who rely on the provision of medical facilities. They are chiefly distinguished by this and their American evangelistic techniques of conversion.

Watch Tower and the Seventh-day Adventists originated in the United States as millenarian sects, but this aspect of their teaching is not emphasized in the teachings of missionaries in Nyasaland. The Seventh-day Adventists are chiefly distinguished, in the minds of the African population, by their observance of Saturday as the Sabbath and this is also a feature of all the Seventh-day Baptist sects, as their name implies.

The doctrine of the Mikalongwe Mission appears little different from that of the industrial missions, and again very similar to the 'orthodox' Baptist teaching. The founder of the Mikalongwe Mission seceded from the Baptist Industrial Mission on personal rather than doctrinal grounds.

Differences of doctrine are often strongly felt by the White mission staff of the various churches and sects, and sometimes by African ministers and pastors. They are not so strongly felt by the lay members of the congregations. This situation is, of course, not peculiar to

---

[2] See pp. 99–100.

DOCTRINES OF THE SECTS

Southern Nyasaland; ecumenical movements in western Europe are usually more enthusiastically supported by the laity than the clergy, who have a more detailed knowledge of the doctrinal issues involved and are also more directly concerned in their implementation. An indication of the strength of feeling surrounding doctrinal differences between some of the White officials in the different Churches of Christ in Nyasaland is given by the poem quoted as Appendix B to this volume. This poem appears at the beginning of a tract, given to me by the leader of the Faithful Church of Christ after a number of them had been sent to him for distribution among his followers. The American supporters of the Faithful Church of Christ do not believe in Sunday schools or in the plurality of communion cups, both niceties of observance which have little or no meaning for the majority of the members of the sect in Mlanje.

With the exception of the Ethiopian Church, which is discussed later in this chapter, the most striking feature of the doctrines of the African sects is that they are virtually identical with those of the White sects from which they have seceded.[3]

The leader of the *Kagulu Ka Nkhosa*, which seceded from the Zambesi Industrial Mission in 1932, was unable to think of any differences in doctrine between his sect and the Zambesi Mission. He was prompted by one of his elders, who stated that women had to wear a covering on their heads when they went into the prayer house in the Zambesi Mission, while women in the *Kagulu ka Nkhosa* had to wear such a covering on their heads all the time. (This is, in fact, done by the majority of women, both Christian and pagan.)

The leader of the Sent of the Holy Ghost Church, which seceded from the Zambesi Mission in 1934, stated explicitly that there were no differences of doctrine between his sect and the Zambesi Mission. They both had the same laws, he stated, but Zambesi Mission did not adhere to them. In 1956 the Sent of the Holy Ghost Church was able to become affiliated with the Pentecostal Holiness Church, an American Pentecostal sect, 'because', the leader stated, 'the churches were the same'.

The leader of the African Nyasa Church also stated that there were no differences in doctrine between his sect and the Nyasa Industrial Mission; it was a personal quarrel involving accusations of witchcraft which led to his secession from the Nyasa Mission.

---

[3] Parrinder notes a similar phenomenon in Nigeria when he states that some of the sects in Ibadan are 'surprisingly orthodox'. (Parrinder, 1953, p. 108.)

38 SECTARIANISM IN SOUTHERN NYASALAND

The doctrines of each of the Seventh-day Baptist sects are virtually identical; ministers in Joshua Chateka's sect stated that in 1930 Alexander Makwinja introduced a new doctrine demanding that women should not wear coverings on their heads, but that they should wear necklaces of beads. Joshua Chateka is reputed to have started an independent sect because he did not believe in this new practice. These differences do not, however, appear to be keenly felt even by ministers of the two sects, who, on the other hand, are generally only too willing to criticize members of the other sect on personal grounds, and it would appear that they were not the reason for secession, but rather introduced afterwards as distinguishing features.

The African Churches of Christ and the Sons of God were formed not as a result of differences of doctrine but over a disagreement with a newly arrived White missionary about the baptism of converts who had been expelled from the Church of Scotland.

All the African sects use the same hymnbook. This book is also used by the Church of Scotland and most European sects. It is published by the Nyasaland Federation of Missions, in which the Church of Scotland and the Dutch Reformed Church are the members with most congregations. African sects in Mlanje have not produced hymns of their own, though the leader of the Faithful Church of Christ stated that he hoped to do so. Sundkler states that the 'Independent Churches' of Zululand all use hymnbooks produced by White missions, but that there is a tendency for each sect to use a selection of hymns which it regards as its own 'property'.[4] The number of hymns used by the Faithful Church of Christ during the course of numerous services which I attended was a small fraction of those in the book, but hymns are chosen by members of the congregation as well as elders and ministers, and hymns which are popular in one sect also appear to be popular in others. Most members of African sects have also previously been members of another religious association, and so there is a tendency for them to choose the hymns which were popular and which they enjoyed singing before they joined an African sect. Occasionally attempts were made by ministers in the African sects to introduce new hymns to their congregation; this, however, did not appear to be very popular with their followers. Thus the development of differences of doctrine does not provide the basis for the secession of African sects. Those differences that do exist appear to

---

[4] Sundkler, 1961, p. 193.

DOCTRINES OF THE SECTS

be a rationalization of secession and a consequence rather than its *raison d'être*. The emphasis of the Protestant Churches and sects upon the use of the Bible enables almost any interpretation of it to be made, and provides the justification for a minor difference over a detail of doctrine, which the leader of a sect may then use as its distinguishing feature.

But, although the explanation of the existence of African sects is not to be found in differences of doctrine, informants do sometimes state that they have changed their allegiance from one religious association to another for this reason.

The leader of a new sect when he secedes takes with him a proportion of the members of the parent body. In order to expand the membership of the new sect efforts are made at proselytizing among members of other religious associations. The Faithful Church of Christ, for instance, which was formed as a result of secession from the African Church of Christ, has drawn most of its present following from former members of several sects and churches. Some cited differences of doctrine as the reason for their change of allegiance, in particular questions of baptism. Several members stated that they had left the Church of Scotland, for instance, because they disagreed with their doctrine of baptism and quoted Matthew iii, 13, 'Then cometh Jesus from Galilee to Jordan unto John, to be baptized of him', to support their case. This quotation, however, appears to support any sect which practises baptism by total immersion, and all the sects do this, both African and White. Leaving the Church of Scotland could be motivated by a belief in baptism by total immersion, but this is insufficient grounds for joining one African sect rather than any other. Again, it seems that the transfer of allegiance is not due to doctrinal factors in any but a small minority of cases, but that doctrinal variations may be quoted afterwards to justify a change which was, in fact, due mainly to other factors, in particular to the struggle for positions of status and prestige. Except in the Ethiopian Church preachers do not generally emphasize the doctrines of their own particular sect; they preach in rather more general terms, stressing the need for obeying church leaders, avoiding witchcraft, attending services regularly, and especially preparing for the 'Day of Judgement'.

Members of a religious group often have differing ideas about its doctrines. In Southern Nyasaland to a certain extent this is a reflection of the different standards of education received by members of one church or sect. An elder in Joshua Chateka's Seventh-day Baptists,

40 SECTARIANISM IN SOUTHERN NYASALAND

for instance, explained the Seventh-day principle by saying that in Nyasaland there were three groups of people, the Whites, the Indians, and the Africans. The Whites celebrated Sunday, the Indians Friday (a reference to Islam), and so the Africans should celebrate Saturday. This explanation was not supported by other informants from this sect, and suggests that people may take part in a particular ritual for a variety of reasons.

The Seventh-day Baptist sects display some elements of African-ism, and many of their members hold similar views to members of the Ethiopian Church about Africans being the 'descendants of Ham',[5] The Seventh-day Baptists also frequently oppose government rules which they find it impossible to support by reference to the Bible. These Africanist sentiments do not, however, play an important part in the doctrines of the other African sects with which I had contact in Mlanje, and do not provide their *raison d'être*.

Sundkler, discussing the 'Bantu Independent Churches' of Zulu-land, suggests that the 'colour bar' is one of the main factors in the development of sectarianism in the Union of South Africa. 'If it is a fact—and I believe that it is,' he states, 'that nowhere else has the Separatist Church movement grown to such dimensions as in the Union of South Africa, this must mean that there is in South African society some particular root cause not found elsewhere, at least to the same extent, which leads to this result. This root cause is the colour line between White and Black.' He continues; '[There is a] discrepancy between the missionary's Christian Message and the Euro-pean's Christian life. This discrepancy is above all revealed in the colour bar within the Christian Church. "Net vir Blankes—For Europeans only" is figuratively but no less virtually written on many church doors in the Union. And this fact is one of the reasons for the emergence of Independent Bantu churches.'[6]

This is not the case in Nyasaland. Apartheid is not a Government policy in the Protectorate. There are no 'Native Reserves'. Demogra-phically Nyasaland is very different from South Africa and the very much smaller ratio of Whites to Africans is significant in this context. The African population of the Protectorate is some 3,000,000, while the European population is some 8,000. Admittedly the ratio of Europeans to Africans is highest in the Southern Province, but even here it is low when compared with the Union of South Africa or with

---

[5] See below, pp. 46–51.   [6] Sundkler, op. cit., pp. 32 and 37.

DOCTRINES OF THE SECTS

the Rhodesias. The religious groups organized by Whites in Nyasaland are primarily missionary associations concerned with the conversion of the African population to their ranks. Church buildings in the urban area are not primarily for White congregations, but are used mainly by Africans.

No leader of an African sect suggested to me that he had started his sect as a result of a colour bar in a White religious group. One Muslim informant, the governor of an Islamic school, felt that Islam was better than Christianity because there were no distinctions of colour in Islam, both Indians and Africans praying together, but this is not an easily justifiable argument in Nyasaland. Nyasaland is not, however, socially isolated from the remainder of Southern Africa; many people have been to the Union of South Africa and to Southern Rhodesia as labour migrants, have seen the 'colour bar' in operation and have told others of their experiences with Whites in these countries. I do not mean to suggest that none of the racialist attitudes found in other parts of Southern Africa are present among the White population of Nyasaland; this is not the case, but the 'settler' population of the country is so small that problems of race relations tend to be less significant than in many other parts of Central and Southern Africa. White missionaries in Nyasaland may indeed frequently be identified by Africans with other Whites in the territory. I have heard minor African National Congress officials suggesting that they should be expelled from the country together with the settlers; this does not, however, seem to have formed the basis of sectarian developments.

During the political disturbances of 1958–9 White missionaries attached to the Church of Scotland did, in fact, openly side with the African National Congress, earning themselves the scorn of some settlers among their urban congregations, and generally finding themselves in opposition to the Government.

Sectarianism occurs in parts of Africa where relations between Whites and Africans are very different from those found in Southern Africa.[7] The relations between Africans and Whites in a particular area appear to be associated with the type of sectarian developments found there, but this is not the sole cause of sectarianism.

The rapid social changes, characteristic of simpler societies which have come into contact with complex and specialized Western culture,

---

[7] See, for instance, Banton, 1956, pp. 56–63, and Parrinder, 1954, Chapter 6, where he discusses the African sects in the Nigerian city of Ibadan.

S.S.N.–D

SECTARIANISM IN SOUTHERN NYASALAND

have frequently been accompanied by the rise of prophets. These prophets often preach a messianic or millenarian message, claiming revelations from the supernatural, either from the Christian God, or from a traditional deity or culture hero. They may claim to be the messiah of their people, or a mouthpiece of the messiah, or they may forecast an impending millennium prophesying a catastrophic change in the existing social order.[8]

In many cases these prophets have been able to gather a following and to start a new religious group with their prophecies forming the core of its doctrine; their followers may be drawn from mission churches or they may be pagans. The religious groups formed by such prophets may well be short-lived if their prophecies are not realized— on the other hand some such groups have survived for many years.

Prophecies of this nature have not provided the basis for sectarianism in Mlanje. Here there are no sects led by prophets claiming to be messiahs or their messengers. In 1958-9 the English term 'messiah' was frequently on the lips of Nyasaland Africans when they were talking about the President of the Nyasaland African National Congress, Dr. Hastings Banda. It is difficult to estimate how far those who used the term considered him to have supernatural power; he was certainly regarded with a great deal of awe and enthusiasm as the saviour of the Nyasaland people. Hobsbawm[9] has pointed out that it may be difficult to disentangle the religious and political elements in revolutionary movements, and suggests that 'between the two extremes of the "pure" millenarian and the "pure" political revolutionary all manner of intermediate positions are possible.' Although some of Dr. Banda's followers with whom I spoke endowed him with supernatural qualities, it seems that we should place him fairly near the political end of this spectrum. He did not become the focus of a new religious group. His followers were drawn from many different churches and sects both White and African, and included many pagans. They remained members of these religious groups and did not change their allegiance. The Nyasaland African National Congress

---

[8] The notion of a messiah is not essential to millenarianism; the North American Ghost Dances and some of the early Cargo Cults such as the Vailala Madness involved millenarian though not messianic prophecies. Similarly it seems that messianic movements need not be millenarian; the Nazarite Church founded by Isiah Shembe in Zululand has as the focus of its doctrine the notion that Isiah Shembe is the 'Black Christ'—the messiah of his people—but there does not appear to be any idea of a rapidly approaching millennium.

[9] Hobsbawm, 1959, p. 59.

DOCTRINES OF THE SECTS

43

was a political party, with some religious overtones. It was not a religious movement and still less was it a sect. Banda nowhere displaced Christ as the focus of religious worship.

Millenarian movements are frequently spoken of as though they were a separate category of religious phenomena, but we should remember that *all* Christian churches are millenarian *in some degree*; all profess a belief in the Second Coming of Christ. Christian churches do, however, differ very greatly in the degree to which they are preoccupied with the millennium. The more firmly established a particular church, the less likely it is to emphasize a future catastrophic change in the social order; it tends to have a vested interest in maintaining the *status quo*. Thus we find that the Roman Catholic Church places the least emphasis on an impending millennium, while the smaller Protestant Churches and sects emphasize it most. I have the impression that the impending millennium was not emphasized any more in sermons in the African sects than in White ones, but I have no quantitative data to substantiate this.

If we restrict the use of the term millenarian to apply only to those religious groups which have as the central feature of their doctrine the notion that a catastrophic change in the social order is rapidly impending, and perhaps a specific date for it fixed, then there were no millenarian sects, so far as I am aware, in Mlanje or Chapananga's area in 1958–9. Two of the White sects in the area originated, however, as movements of this type. The Watch Tower or Jehovah's Witnesses started in the latter half of the last century as a result of prophecies by Charles Taze Russell that the millennium would arrive in 1914. When Watch Tower literature was distributed in Nyasaland from South Africa in the years before 1914, it caused considerable consternation to the Government, who saw the movement as a source of potential subversive activities. Though the idea that the millennium is still fairly evident is part of their teaching, the Watch Tower movement has become 'respectable' in Nyasaland; no longer is it regarded as a potential source of subversion. The emphasis in its doctrines seems to have shifted to other aspects of Christ's teaching. This seems parallel to developments in Christianity as a whole. The notion of the *parousia* or Second Coming of Christ seems to have played an important part in the teachings of the early Church, but gradually the emphasis in the established churches has shifted to other aspects of Christ's teaching, when it was realized that the Second Coming was not so imminent as had been thought. Throughout the history of

44 SECTARIANISM IN SOUTHERN NYASALAND

Christianity the gospels have periodically been interpreted to show that the millennium is imminent, and this has given rise to the development of groups such as the Jehovah's Witnesses. If such groups are to survive, then they must either consider that the millennium in some form or other has arrived when they prophesied that it would, or this part of their teaching must be dropped.

The early history of the Seventh-day Adventists, as their name implies, was associated with teachings about the imminent return of Christ, this time in 1874. When it was found that the prophecy was not fulfilled—the emphasis here also moved to other aspects of their doctrine, in this case the particular stress on the Seventh-day principle. The Seventh-day Adventists were less millenarian, in the narrow sense of the term, than Watch Tower when they started missionary work in Nyasaland.

Although messianism or millenarianism has not provided the basis for the formation of African sects or religious movements in Mlanje or Chapananga's area, statements of a millenarian nature gave rise to rumours during my fieldwork in 1958–9. In a large village in Chapananga's area where I had been living for some time, carrying out a detailed village census and constructing genealogies, a rumour arose that the end of the world was imminent, and that it would be preceded by another flood, similar to the one endured by Noah. It was my task to write a new Nyanja Bible which would survive the flood and would tell how the people of the 'antediluvian' Nyasaland had been related. Informants were well aware of the large number of genealogies to be found in the Old Testament. It was with some reluctance that I denied the rumour and thus forewent the opportunity to create an experimental situation by attempting to be the centre of a new sect.

In Nazombe's area in March 1959 shortly after the 'Declaration of a State of Emergency', when aircraft were flying overhead on reconnaissance flights and distributing leaflets, and troops were known to be in the vicinity, I recorded another millenarian rumour. Quoting Revelations xvii. 10. ('And there are seven kings, five are fallen and one is, and the other is not yet come, and when he cometh he must continue a short space'), it was suggested that the end of the world was near at hand because George VI was the sixth king, and Elizabeth was thus the seventh and last. This rumour appeared to have been started by a teacher in a nearby Church of Scotland; it was not widely accepted and did not form the basis, so far as I am aware, for any social action and certainly not in the formation of a new sect.

DOCTRINES OF THE SECTS

The millenarian idea is thus found in Southern Nyasaland, based upon an interpretation of the Bible rather than direct revelation from the divine. Prophecy, however, seems to have played little part in the traditional organization of the area, and this may partly account for the apparent absence of influential contemporary prophets. A Northern Rhodesian prophetess, Alice Lenshina, who seceded from the Church of Scotland and founded the Lumpa Church,[10] now has a large following in Northern Rhodesia and parts of Nyasaland, but her influence does not extend either to Chapanaga's area or Mlanje.

A characteristic of sectarianism in Zululand has been the proliferation of sects and prophets emphasizing faith healing. These are the 'independent churches' which Sundkler classifies as Zionist,[11] suggesting that the emphasis on healing is the central theme of their doctrine. Faith healing is not highly developed in any of the African sects with which I had contact in Mlanje. It may be more important in two other African sects in the area, the Watchman Healing Mission and the Zion Restoration Church, but I have no first-hand details of their practices, which are said to have been introduced from South Africa by returning labour migrants. The Assemblies of God, a White sect with American missionaries resident in Nyasaland, expresses a belief in the power of faith healing, and this is the theme in a number of Nyanja tracts distributed to the congregations. Healing is not, however, the central tenet of the doctrine of the Assemblies of God as it is in the Zionist sects in Zululand. The missionary in charge of the sect in Southern Nyasaland felt that some of his colleagues over-emphasized spiritual healing, and he himself encouraged members of the sect to take advantage of medical facilities provided by the Government. Conversations with African members of this sect did not reveal that they generally held any very different opinions about spiritual healing from members of other sects. Divine healing is often associated with baptism by total immersion. As all the sects in southern Nyasaland practice this type of baptism, it is perhaps surprising that so little emphasis is laid on spiritual healing. There are a number of possible reasons for this. Traditional healing practices do not seem to have been so closely integrated with the traditional religious beliefs as appears to have been the case among the Zulu; secondly, among the Zulu many of the prophets have congregations consisting to a large extent of barren women desiring children; while

---

[10] See Rotberg, 1961, pp. 63–79.   [11] Sundkler, op. cit., Chapter 6.

46 SECTARIANISM IN SOUTHERN NYASALAND

children are certainly desired in Southern Nyasaland, there does not appear to be the same stigma attached to a barren woman as there is in Zululand. Almost all the population of Mlanje, and to a lesser extent of Chapananga's area, is within reach of a dispensary and of Government medical facilities, and these are frequented by large numbers of people. Finally, and I think probably most important, the African sects in this area are essentially replicas of the mission churches from which they have seceded, with the exception of the Ethiopian Church, and of these missions only the Assemblies of God emphasizes faith healing and there have been no secessions from this sect.

We must look beyond differences of doctrine if we are to understand sectarianism in Southern Nyasaland. The reasons for the African sects being replicas of the mission sects from which they have seceded will, I hope, become apparent in later chapters; meanwhile, I describe the doctrine of the one African sect which has introduced radically different doctrines—the Ethiopian Church.

The Ethiopian Church: a synthetist sect

Linton has introduced the term 'Nativistic Movement' to refer to 'any conscious organized attempt on the part of a society's members to revive or perpetuate selected aspects of its culture.'[12] Many religious movements which have arisen in times of rapid social change fit into this category, but after the term had been introduced there was a tendency for it to be applied to almost any religious movement arising in such times. More recently efforts have been made by Wallace,[13] Smith,[14] Köbben,[15] and others to refine the notion of nativistic and to suggest new categories of religious movements.

In a discussion of the Ethiopian Church in Southern Nyasaland Smith's classification seems the most apposite. She defines the term nativistic in the same way as Linton, but uses it as part of a tri-partite classification of 'cult movements'; the other types of her classification 'vitalistic movements', which she defines as 'any conscious organized attempt on the part of a society's members to incorporate in its culture selected aspects of a culture in contact with it', and 'synthetist movements' as 'any conscious organized attempt on the part of a society's members to combine selected aspects of two cultures'. It is

---

[12] Linton, 1943, pp. 230–9. [13] Wallace, 1956, pp. 264–81.
[14] Smith, 1959. [15] Köbben, 1960, pp. 117–63.

DOCTRINES OF THE SECTS

the aim of these movements, not their content, which is critical in Smith's classification; all involve the selection of certain aspects of the traditional culture; nativistic movements emphasize the perpetuation or revival of these aspects, vitalistic ones emphasize the acceptance of *certain* aspects of the new culture, and synthetist movements emphasize the combination of selected aspects of each.

The Ethiopian Church in Southern Nyasaland falls into the synthetist category. Although the nativistic element is emphasized, particularly by outsiders, in the name by which it is popularly known— The *Calici ca Makolo*—'The Church of the Ancestors', its doctrines are a conscious and organized attempt to combine the traditional magico-religious beliefs of the area with some of the doctrines introduced by the Protestant missions.

This sect was founded at Ncheu in the Central Province by Peter Nyambo, an Ngoni, and ex-Seventh-day Adventist who spent many years in the Union of South Africa, returning to Nyasaland in 1942.[16] The title 'Ethiopian Church' appears to be of South African origin, but the sect has no formal links with those with a similar name in South Africa; it is an autonomous body in the Protectorate, although some of the doctrines are probably of South African origin.

Informants who are members of this sect stress the need for retaining the 'ways of the ancestors' (*macitidwe wa makolo*). Passages from the Old Testament in which reference is made to ancestors, forebears and forefathers, are frequently quoted in sermons and in discussion. The need for the Hebrews to retain the ways of their ancestors is taken as applying equally well to the Africans, and members of this sect criticize White missionaries for ignoring these passages and cheating them. The following passages are amongst those which preachers used as texts for sermons which I heard: Deuteronomy xxxii. 7, 'Remember the days of old, consider the years of many generations, ask thy father and he will show thee, ask the elders and they will tell thee'; Malachi ii. 10, 'Have we not all one Father? Hath not God created us? Why do we deal treacherously every man against his brother by profaning the covenant of our fathers?'; Job viii. 8, 'For inquire, I pray thee, of the former age, and prepare thyself for the search of their fathers.' The widow of a Nguru village headman who was a member of this sect, when invited by the preacher to speak during a service, told how the younger generation only wanted to become like the

---

[16] For further details see Shepperson and Price, 1958, pp. 203–9.

48   SECTARIANISM IN SOUTHERN NYASALAND

Whites and were forgetting the ways of their ancestors. She said, for instance, that their ancestors would not have intercourse with their wives during menstruation and that the present ignorance of this rule was responsible for much of the disease in the country.

Preachers and other members of the sect stressed particularly the importance of the ancestral spirits, and making the appropriate offerings to them. This, too, was justified with reference to the Old Testament, Leviticus ii. 14; 'And if thou offer a meat offering of thy first fruits unto the Lord, thou shalt offer for a meat offering of thy first fruits, green ears of corn, dried by the fire, even corn beaten out of full ears.' The preacher told his congregation that the injunction was to make an offering of flour (*ufa*) exactly as their own ancestors had done. Such offerings in the Ethiopian Church, he told me afterwards, should be made annually by the minister at the time of the harvest, but at all other times should be made by the *mwini mbumba* in the traditional way. Another minister later suggested that the communion bread was the White's form of offering to their ancestors; the fact that it was consumed made no difference.

Preachers also emphasized the importance of supplicating the ancestral spirits for rain. They suggested that the Whites do this, but that their ancestors will not help the Africans. One preacher drew an analogy with a letter, stating that if a person sends a letter he must address it correctly otherwise it will not arrive; similarly if offerings are made to the ancestors for rain, then they must be made to the right ancestors. Emphasizing the importance of rain rituals stresses the importance of the office of *mwini dziko* (the 'owner' of the country), who is responsible for their performance; only the spirits of his matrilineage have the power to send rain. Traditionally the *mwini dziko* was the chief; today the two functions have in some instances been separated (this is the case in N. A. Nazombe's area, where his mother's brother is the *mwini dziko*). The Ethiopian Church then emphasizes the importance of the chief and his matrilineage, and it is significant that it was invited to form a congregation in his village by village headman Ntepha shortly after a court case in which he was alleged to have performed the rain rituals as though he were *mwini dziko* of Nazombe's area. Nazombe himself is a Roman Catholic, and gave the Ethiopian Church no support. Ntepha, however, had some claim to being a *mwini dziko*, and this was recognized by the Ethiopians.[17]

---

[17] I have analysed this case in detail, in Wishlade, 1961, pp. 36–45; also see below, pp. 92–4.

DOCTRINES OF THE SECTS

49

An important element in the doctrine and teaching of the Ethiopian Church is the rejection of many of the rules of the other Christian religious associations. Other Protestant Christian associations prohibit beer-brewing and drinking and polygyny, though the rules are of course not always kept. The Ethiopian Church rejects the injunction against drinking beer, again with Biblical justification—Luke vii. 34, 'The Son of Man is come eating and drinking'. Preachers stated that members of the sect should attend services on a Sunday, but thereafter they may drink beer. Several members of the sect condemned the Church of Scotland for having a rule against drinking beer which everyone knew was not kept, except when the European missionary paid them a visit. One member stated pithily, *Sali Kuopa Mulungu iai, ali Kuopa anthu basi*, 'They are not afraid of God, they are only afraid of men.' He went on to say that if a member of the Church of Scotland reported another for drinking, then he would be made a deacon. The Ethiopian Church permits, and even encourages polygyny, a practice which is categorically condemned by all the other churches and sects. They frequently cite the ancient Hebrews, who are recorded in the Old Testament as having more than one wife, to justify their practice. The rejection of the rules of the other churches and sects has led to the Ethiopian Church being dubbed by outsiders—the *Zoipa Citani* ('Do Bad Things') Church.[18]

There is a general belief amongst the members of the Ethiopian Church that the European missionaries are hoodwinking the Africans, that they are only teaching them parts of the Bible and deliberately withholding others. The emphasis placed upon the Bible is as strong in this sect as in any other, and sermons may contain as many as sixteen separate quotations from it, but the majority are from the Old Testament. Sermons in the Ethiopian Church follow the same pattern as those in other sects, consisting of numerous texts each followed by a brief exposition. After one service the preacher at a newly formed congregation asked for questions and was heckled by a member of the Church of Scotland asking for his comments on various passages of scripture referring to the Day of Judgement. These questions were answered by the preacher by reference to further passages of scripture, and the discussion developed into an opportunity for the heckler

---

[18] See 'Sinners are Saints in "Do What You Like Church",' an article in the *Sunday Mail* published in Salisbury (Southern Rhodesia) on 19 February 1961, which stresses this aspect of the Ethiopian Church to the exclusion of all others. I am very grateful to Professor J. C. Mitchell for drawing my attention to this article.

50   SECTARIANISM IN SOUTHERN NYASALAND

and the preacher to display their not inconsiderable ability to quote the chapter and verse of passages which they thought relevant.

Not only is the same translation of the Bible used in sermons and teaching in the Ethiopian Church, but the hymn-book which they use is the one published by the Nyasaland Federation of Missions and used in most other churches and sects. Preachers and members of Ethiopian congregations choose hymns from this book—apparently with little or no regard for the doctrinal implications of the words.

A considerable amount of anti-White feeling was expressed in the teachings of the Ethiopian preachers whom I met. My contact with this sect, however, was at a time when relations between Whites and Africans in Nyasaland were particularly tense, and it is possible that these 'Africanist' sentiments played a larger part in the teachings of the sect than they would have done at any other time. The Ethiopian Church was not considered by the administration in Ncheu, where it has its headquarters, to be associated with any political activities of a subversive nature, but rather to be one of the most 'respectable' of the African sects in the District. The expression of Africanist sentiments in the congregations with which I had contact may have been a local, and possibly transitory, phenomenon, and not typical of the sect as a whole.[19]

Although sermons in all the churches and sects are habitually given in Nyanja, which is understood by all the congregation, on several occasions preachers in the Ethiopian Church switched in the middle of a sermon into Nguru. This was obviously designed to prevent me, as a White, from understanding what was being said. In these cases I was able to get only a verbal résumé of the sermon from my assistant, who was neither fluent in Nguru nor literate, after the service. The following text was used in a sermon part of which was given in Nguru: Deuteronomy xxviii. 48–49, 'Therefore shalt thou serve thine enemies which the Lord shall send against thee in hunger and thirst, and in nakedness, and in want of all things, and he shall put a yoke of iron upon thy neck, until he hath destroyed thee. The Lord shall bring a nation against thee from afar, from the end of the earth, as swift as the eagle flieth, a nation whose tongue thou shalt not understand.' The parallel between the tribulations of the Hebrews, and the tribulations

---

[19] My information on the Ethiopian Church is drawn entirely from congregations in Mlanje District. I had made arrangements to meet the leader of the sect, Peter Nyambo, at Ncheu, but unfortunately was prevented by illness from fulfilling them.

DOCTRINES OF THE SECTS

of the Africans under White rule has not gone unnoticed in other parts of Africa.[20]

One text was particularly apposite to the local situation at the time and was read with great emphasis by the preacher at a service shortly after an incident which resulted in a nearby village headman, Misomali, being sent to prison. A number of women from Misomali's village had gone to the forest reserve without permits (which cost 3d. and are obtained from the Native Authority office) to collect firewood. Challenged by the Forestry Department's guard they ran away and returned to the village. Misomali and several men from his village then attacked the forest guard and Misomali was subsequently convicted at the Native Authority Court. The text comes from Lamentations v. 1–5: 'Remember, O Lord, what is come upon us; consider and behold our reproach. Our inheritance is turned unto strangers, our houses to aliens. We are orphans and fatherless, our mothers are widows. We have drunken water for money; *our wood is sold unto us.*'

Members of the sect emphasized that the Whites had introduced many rules for which there was no justification in the Bible—rules about the construction of ridges to prevent soil erosion, and the digging of latrines.

The identification of Africans with the descendants of Ham, who was cursed by his father Noah, has a long history. This doctrine is not held by any of the White missions in Nyasaland, who all teach the equality of all men in the sight of God; it is, however, a corner-stone of the doctrine of the Dutch Reformed Church in South Africa and is part of the mythical charter for their race relations policy. The same doctrine also figures in the teachings of many Ethiopian Churches in South Africa.[21] One preacher in the Ethiopian Church in Nyasaland, discussing points of doctrine with members of the congregation after a service, told his audience that the Africans were the descendants of Ham, Cush, and Nimrod, and referred them to Genesis x. 6–9. However, he made no reference to the myth that Ham and his descendants were cursed by Noah. He pointed out rather that Ham, Cush, and Nimrod were good men and had killed no man, defying any of his listeners to show him in the Bible a statement that they had. The emphasis on their descent from Ham is a charter for the unity of Africans *vis-à-vis* the Whites, it shows that they have a position in the divine creation as ancient as the Whites and that they are just as much

---

[20] See, for instance, Sundkler, 1961, p. 277.   [21] Sundkler, op. cit., p. 333.

52 SECTARIANISM IN SOUTHERN NYASALAND

God's 'chosen people'. There is no need for shame in admitting descent from Ham; the curse placed on him, if it is considered at all, does not seem to be thought of as applying to his descendants. They do not consider that this doctrine relegates them to the position of hewers of wood and drawers of water for all time.

In common with the Ethiopian sects in South Africa, the Ethiopian Church in Nyasaland equates Ethiopia with Africa as a whole.[22] Biblical references to Ethiopia and Ethiopians are taken as applying to all Africans. In one sermon a preacher quoted Isaiah xx. 4 as illustrating their plight: 'So shall the king of the Assyrians lead away the Egyptian prisoners and the Ethiopian captives, young and old, naked and barefoot, even with their buttocks uncovered to the shame of the Egyptians.'

Although much of the teaching of the Whites was specifically rejected and Africanist sentiments expressed and given Biblical support, the Ethiopian Church in Mlanje in 1958–9 was not a major focus of anti-White activities; this was the role of Nyasaland African National Congress. When Congress was proscribed and many of its officials imprisoned in March 1959, the Ethiopian Church expanded rapidly in parts of the District and several new congregations were established. Its influence in the District as a whole, however, remained slight. According to one account this expansion seems to have continued and a more recent guess, though probably not a very inspired one, puts the number of followers at 'between 8,000 and 10,000 in the Cholo–Mlanje–Zomba area of the Southern Province,[23] but there is still no indication that 'Ethiopianism' is a major force in the contemporary social and religious scene in Nyasaland.

---

[22] Ibid., p. 57.   [23] *Sunday Mail*, 19 February 1961.

V

RITUAL AND WORSHIP

EVERY established congregation has its own church building or
prayer house in which it holds all its services, apart from parts of
the baptismal service, held on the nearest river bank, and
funerals. Most prayer houses are made from wattle and daub and have
a thatched roof, though some, usually those belonging to larger
congregations, are built of Kimberley brick and a few have corrugated
iron roofs. Unglazed 'windows' are left in the walls to allow the entry
of light and air. Neither the congregation nor its officials are recognized by outsiders until some sort of building has been erected, but
some newly formed congregations erect temporary buildings of grass
until they have accumulated sufficient resources to build a more permanent structure. The size of church buildings varies considerably,
but the layout of those belonging to Protestant congregations is
basically similar. The buildings are rectangular with a door at one end
and a raised platform at the other; usually no attempt is made to place
this platform at the east of the building. A plain wooden table stands
on the platform, and during services this may be covered with a white
cloth; the officiant, together with the elders of the congregation and
perhaps a deaconess, sit behind this table, facing the remainder of the
congregation.

These officials sit on chairs or benches which, like the table, in
many cases have been borrowed from the houses of members of the
congregation living nearby. This is all the furniture to be found in
most prayer houses, and there is no form of decoration, carving or
pictures on any of the walls. The congregation sit on raised benches
made of mud, men usually on one side of the main aisle and women on
the other—though this custom is not strictly observed if the building
is full and there is a shortage of seats on one side.

The weekly service

All the churches and sects, except the Seventh-day Adventists and
the Seventh-day Baptists, hold their main services each week on a
Sunday. About noon, or shortly before, the congregation are summoned to the service by a bell, which may be rung for anything up to
half an hour before the service begins. A very effective bell is often

54 SECTARIANISM IN SOUTHERN NYASALAND

made by suspending a discarded lorry brake drum from a branch of a tree on a length or rope and striking it with a bolt. Some of the congregation, who have walked or cycled some distance, may already have arrived and be sitting in small groups chatting outside the prayer house. Gradually the congregation enters the building, in some congregations the men waiting outside until all the women have taken their places inside—this seems to be characteristic of particular congregations rather than particular sects.

The members of the congregation attending the service don their 'Sunday best' clothes, the women wearing their newest dresses and with scarves on their heads and some of them carrying umbrellas. The men, too, put on their best clothes and those who possess them proudly carry their Bibles into the prayer house.

The pattern of the service in all the congregations, except those belonging to the Roman Catholic Church, is essentially similar; the services in the Ethiopian Church are distinguished by the content of the sermon rather than by variations in the pattern of the service. Before the formal service starts individual members of the congregation choose a hymn, call out its number and those present sing it sitting down. I suggested in Chapter IV, that there appeared to be little correlation between the hymns chosen and the sect to which the congregation belongs. This is possibly the result of the high mobility of Christians from one sect to another. After two or three hymns have been sung in this way the preacher himself stands and announces the number of another one; this marks the beginning of the formal service and the congregation rises to sing. The officiant then makes a fairly lengthy extempore prayer, usually including an opportunity for the silent confession of sins by members of the congregation and a request for absolution. He asks for blessings on members of the congregation, particularly those who are sick, who may be mentioned personally by name, though they are not usually present at the service and no attempt is made to perform any healing ritual for them. He asks for blessings on absent labour migrants, for the head of the sect and its officials, frequently he asks for blessings on the Queen, and the Governor of Nyasaland—this occurs in both African and White sects. He also usually includes a request for favourable weather for crops and gives thanks for blessings which have already been received. At the end of this prayer the preacher starts the Lord's Prayer, which is repeated by the whole congregation. This is followed by another hymn. The officiant, or one of the elders of the congregation able to

RITUAL AND WORSHIP

do so, then reads a passage of scripture. At some services I attended where an elder did this the reading was punctuated by a grunt of approval from the preacher at the end of every verse. The choice of the passage lies with the pastor in charge of the congregation, or occasionally with a visiting preacher: there is no set lesson laid down in a lectionary as there is in the Roman Catholic Church. This may be followed by another hymn, or directly by the sermon. The sermon is the central feature of the service in all the Protestant congregations and consists of a number of scriptural quotations, each followed by an exposition. Sometimes I heard as many as sixteen separate passages of scripture read, either by the preacher himself or one of the elders. If they are being read by an elder, the preacher will often interrupt him in the middle of a sentence in order to make another point. Sometimes the preacher himself is interrupted by a member of the congregation who starts to sing a hymn; the remainder of the congregation soon join in and the preacher is forced to a standstill, only to resume again undaunted after the last verse has been sung. It is not uncommon, particularly in African sects, for there to be two sermons, separated by a hymn, by two different preachers. This results in the service lasting anything up to two hours, most of which is spent in preaching. Almost all the sermons I heard, except those given by senior officials and White missionaries of the White sects and the Church of Scotland, showed little evidence of advance preparation. There is generally no distinguishable theme running right through; they are more in the nature of extempore expositions of scriptural texts and are frequently very repetitive. Most sermons emphasize the necessity for observing God's law and renouncing the ways of the pagans. The emphasis on law and correct ethical behaviour is very strong in both White and African sects. Some, but by no means all, preachers become emotionally excited during their preaching, but I saw little evidence of members of their congregations becoming similarly affected. After the sermon another hymn follows and then a short extempore prayer which includes a formal blessing.

The Assemblies of God services follow a similar pattern, but on one occasion, when the officiant was a White American missionary, the service assumed the character of a 'revivalist meeting'. The missionary was accompanied by his wife playing an accordion and they punctuated the singing of the hymns with loud 'Alleluias'. At this service the missionary adopted the 'revivalist' practice, at the end of his sermon, of asking all those who 'loved Christ' to raise their hands.

56 SECTARIANISM IN SOUTHERN NYASALAND

This, however, appeared to be an unfamiliar technique and no hands were raised. I did not see such techniques employed at any other services.

The services of the Protestant churches and sects, both those under African and those under European leadership, are characterized by the lack of ritual and symbolism, and by the extent to which the choice of passages of scripture, the subject of the sermon, and the content of the extempore prayers are left to the individual preacher. The services of the Roman Catholic Church are in complete contrast to this. At Catholic mission stations, where one or more priests are resident, Mass is celebrated daily according to the rites which are universal in this Church. In the outlying congregations where no priest is resident, Mass cannot be celebrated, and the service which is held on a Sunday is taken by a lay catechist. The form of this service is clearly laid down in a book which most literate Catholics possess. There is little room for individual variations and there are no extempore prayers. The passages of scripture appointed to be read are laid down in a lectionary and not left to the discretion of the officiant. The sermon is much shorter than in the Protestant sects and is not the main focus of the service. Repetitive chanting plays an important part in the ritual of the Roman Catholic services, but is completely absent from the others. Clearly the Protestant pastor in charge of a congregation has a much greater degree of autonomy than his Roman Catholic counterpart—the lay catechist.

In the Church of Scotland and most sects the Eucharist is celebrated only infrequently at each congregation. This is partly in accordance with the doctrines of the parent bodies of many White missions, and partly because many congregations are in the care of an official not high enough in the ecclesiastical hierarchy to be entitled to celebrate. In a few sects though, notably the Faithful Church of Christ, the Eucharist is celebrated more frequently, often at the end of the weekly service. In the Faithful Church of Christ elders are entitled to celebrate and little ritual surrounds the service; it is regarded purely as a memorial service and neither officials nor members of the sect hold any doctrines of transubstantiation or consubstantiation.

Occasionally services following the pattern of the Sunday service may also be held during the week. Such services are held when an important official of the sect visits the congregation and wishes to preach. In some sects mid-week services especially intended for

RITUAL AND WORSHIP

women are also held; these, too, follow the pattern of the Sunday services. Other mid-week activities include Bible classes which, in the churches and some of the sects, are a necessary preliminary to baptism.

Baptism

In all the sects baptism is by total immersion, in contrast to the Church of Scotland and the Roman Catholic Church, where a token sprinkling of water suffices. It is in their baptismal services that ritual and symbolism are most highly developed in the Protestant sects. The following description of a baptismal service, which I attended at a congregation of the Faithful Church of Christ, is typical of others, except that the questions asked of the candidates vary from one sect to another and differ particularly in those sects which examine their candidates for a knowledge of the fundamentals of the Christian faith before baptism.

This is a new congregation, recently established in Nankuku village in Zomba District. They have not yet had time to erect a permanent prayer house. Members of the congregation start to assemble, together with visitors from other congregations, outside their grass prayer house around 11 a.m. They sing hymns while they wait for others to arrive. All those expected have now arrived and the head of the sect (the Rev. E. C. Severe), two ministers, and those male members of the congregation who possess bicycles ride to the bank of the river about a mile away. The rest of the congregation walk there singing hymns as they go. More hymns are sung on the river bank and then Severe preaches a short sermon on the meaning of baptism.

There are four candidates at this service, a girl about 16 years old, two boys slightly older than her and one younger. All are dressed in old clothes and the boys are each accompanied by a deacon and the girl by a deaconess.

At the end of the sermon the male members of the congregation and the two ministers wade out to a sand-bank in the middle of the river, while the women and the candidates and the officials accompanying them remain on the bank. Severe also stays at the water's edge, saying (to me) that the river is infested with *likodzo* (bilharzia). The candidates come one by one to Severe who asks them:

'*Kodi ukhulupirira kuti Jesu Kristu ndi Mwana wa Mulungu wa Moyo?*' (Do you believe that Jesus Christ is the Son of the Living God?)

'*Kodi ukhulupirira kuti adzakupulumitsa pa tsiku lomaliza?*' (Do you believe that He will save you on the last day?)

58 SECTARIANISM IN SOUTHERN NYASALAND

'*Kodi ukhulupirira kuti adzakulanga pa tsiku lomaliza ngati ubwelela mbuyo?*' (Do you believe that He will punish you on the last day if you go back [from the Christian way]?)

The candidates each answer '*Inde*' (Yes) and are admonished .

'*Ngati ukhulupirira conco khala wodala kufikira Iye akadza.*' (If you believe this, remain faithful until He comes.)

The congregation now sings another hymn and during this the candidates one by one wade out to the minister standing in the middle of the river. Supporting them under their backs he immerses them completely in the water. They then make their way back to the bank where they are met by the deacon or deaconess accompanying them. These acolytes have charge of the candidates' best clothes and they retire to the bush with them to help them put them on. By the time they return to the river bank the congregation is beginning to return, in twos and threes, to the prayer house. The visitors remain to take food with the pastor in charge of the congregation at his house, while the candidates and the rest of the congregation disperse.

Sometimes baptismal services are held immediately before the weekly service and so instead of dispersing the candidates and congregation return to the prayer house for the service.

Baptism in all the sects symbolizes entry into it. It symbolizes the transition of a person from being a *wakunja* (someone outside [the Church] i.e. a pagan) to being a Christian. It is a 'rite de passage', albeit a short one, and one where the actual rites of transition appear to be undeveloped. The immersion in the river is clearly regarded as a rite of separation; the candidate symbolically separates himself from his past life and his sins are washed away in the water. The attendance of the candidates at the service which follows, either directly after the baptism or on the following Sunday, marks their incorporation into the sect when they are welcomed by the preacher.

I have no evidence to suggest that members and officials of African sects interpret baptism in a different way from those in White sects (though I have not witnessed a baptismal service in the Ethiopian Church). Certainly baptism by total immersion in a White sect qualifies a person for membership of an African sect; there is no need for them to be baptized again. The same applies to people changing their allegiance from one African sect to another. On the other hand, officials of African sects are very conscious that the Roman Catholics and Church of Scotland do not practise baptism by total immersion, and insist that those joining them from these churches should be re-baptized.

RITUAL AND WORSHIP

Ritual associated with life crises

Birth

There is no ritual recognition of birth in the African sects.

Marriage

Occasionally marriages are solemnized by a religious ceremony, but this is comparatively rare even among active Christians. Many ministers whom I met had not been married according to Christian rites.[1] I have not witnessed a marriage ceremony in either a White or an African sect, nor are many marriages registered under the Marriage Ordinance in either Mlanje or Chapananga's area. Marriage in Southern Nyasaland is not the occasion for elaborate ceremonial in either the traditional or the contemporary situation.[2]

Death

When active Christians die they are buried in accordance with Christian funeral rites. The following description is of a funeral which I attended in the Faithful Church of Christ, the African sect with which I am most familiar.

James, the five-year-old son of Cipolopolo, a minister in the Faithful Church of Christ at Chaima village in Zomba District, is sick. His father goes and informs his wife's mother's brother, who is the child's *mwini mbumba*[3] and the boy is given African medicine. This is unsuccessful and the child dies two days later about nine o'clock in the morning. Another minister in the congregation, Chimenya, comes and informs Severe, the head of the sect who was visiting nearby at the time of the death, and then slowly tolls the bell outside the prayer house to announce the news to the rest of the congregation. The message is passed round to members of the congregation and to kin that the funeral will be tomorrow, and a member of the congregation who is a carpenter sets to work making a coffin.

The following day people gather at Chipolopolo's house and at his wife's sister's house adjacent. Some wailing can be heard. As it is raining heavily visitors congregate inside the houses and under the verandas; as they arrive they put a penny in a bowl placed under the veranda for contributions

---

[1] Writing of the Northern Rhodesian Copperbelt, Taylor and Lehmann also note that 'the Free Churches seem to have very few of their marriages celebrated in church'. (Taylor and Lehmann, 1961, p. 111.)

[2] For a fuller description of the significance of marriage and marriage regulations for sectarianism see below, pp. 112–15

[3] See p. 103.

60   SECTARIANISM IN SOUTHERN NYASALAND

towards the funeral expenses, particularly to provide food for those who
have travelled some distance. While they are waiting in and around the
houses the congregation sings hymns, and as the rain ceases the coffin is
brought outside. It is carried by two male members of the congregation
who are neither relatives of the child nor officials of the congregation, and
placed in the cleared area which surrounds the homestead. The people
also come outside and sit down, the women separately from the men. They
sing two hymns which Chimenya follows with an extempore prayer. A
visiting minister[4] then preaches a sermon, telling the congregation that
they will all die at some time and that they should be ready for death by
always keeping God's laws. Another hymn and extempore prayer follow.
After this those present go in procession to the graveyard about a quarter
of a mile away; they are led by two deaconesses who are followed by two
deacons bearing the coffin. The coffin is placed at the side of the grave
which has already been dug by male members of the congregation. When
all have arrived at the graveside more hymns are sung and another sermon
is preached, this time by Chimenya. After this sermon the coffin is lowered
into the grave on to a mat—which is folded over the lid (this is said by
informants to prevent the soil from spoiling the coffin). To the accompani-
ment of hymns the grave is filled, and then a blessing is given and those
present disperse, the visitors to take food at Chipolopolo's house.

About a hundred people came to the graveside, including members
of the Faithful Church of Christ and kin of the dead child. Christian
and pagans sat together at the funeral; only segregation on the basis
of sex was apparent. All arrangements for the funeral were, however,
made by members of the local congregation. At the funerals of active
Christians (or their young children) the church or sect is the most
significant social group, though people linked to the deceased by
other social ties, such as those of kinship, personal friendship or
residence nearby may also attend the ritual.

The child's father, Chipolopolo, despite his position as a minister,
played no part in the funeral, but merely sat at the side of the grave
on top of an anthill watching. Close relatives do not take an active
part in pagan funeral rites in Southern Nyasaland. Burials are carried
out by burial partners (*adzukulu*), who stand in a permanent reciprocal relationship to the matrilineage of the people they bury.[5] In

---

[4] Severe told me that he himself was expected to preach at this service, but that
he had to return to the headquarters of the sect at Wendewende before it could begin.

[5] In the past, informants stated, the *adzukulu* were appointed on the basis of clan
membership. Today this is no longer the case; they can be anyone at all. The
institution of burial partners is common amongst Central Bantu. (See Stefaniszyn,
1950, and Richards, 1937.)

RITUAL AND WORSHIP

Christian funeral rites minor ecclesiastical officials, usually deacons, have taken the place of the *adzukulu*. They do not stand in the same formal joking relationship with those whom they bury, but they are responsible for digging the grave, bearing the coffin and burying it.

Some other traditional pagan elements are also retained in Protestant funeral rituals. Despite objections from ministers, wailing, for instance, marked the death of Chipolopolo's son, and both Christian and pagan women took part. Sometimes, too, the house of an adult Christian is demolished on death, a traditional pagan practice which on occasion militates against the building of more permanent and costly dwelling-houses. On the other hand, other traditional pagan practices are not observed, except by members of the Ethiopian Church. Traditionally, for instance, close relatives of the deceased shaved their heads as a sign of mourning: this is not always done by pagans today, and I have never seen it done by Christians. Informants suggested, too, that the traditional restrictions on sexual intercourse were not generally observed by Christian mourners.

VI

THE OFFICIALS OF THE SECTS

CHURCHES and sects, in common with other social groups, must have a formalized social structure if they are to remain in existence over a period of time. This chapter is concerned with the pattern of authority in the sects and the way in which they are administered.

We saw in Chapter IV that African sects are not distinguished doctrinally from the White sects from which they seceded; what distinguishes them is the fact that they are completely independent and autonomous social groups. The *Kagulu ka Nkhosa*, for instance, has a similar doctrine, and indeed a similar pattern of authority, to the Zambesi Mission from which it seceded, but it is a separate, independent social unit.

The ecclesiastical structure of all the sects and of the Church of Scotland is very similar, but very different from the Roman Catholic Church with its doctrine of Apostolic Succession. Some of the fundamental differences between African Catholic and Protestant officials have been well stated by F. B. Welbourn in his account of some African sects in Uganda and Kenya: 'The Roman Catholic Church has a priesthood trained at every point to equality with their European colleagues and guiding a flock whose freedom is rigidly controlled; and all find their ecclesiastical focus in Rome. On the other hand, Protestants, aiming at the ultimate development of national churches, use large numbers of poorly trained clergy and lay-readers, taking to every man the open Bible. This in Latin countries is seen as the main source, not only of heresy, but of sedition'.[1]

In all the religious associations in Southern Nyasaland, including the Roman Catholic Church, ecclesiastics (I use this term to denote officials of any church or sect) have functionally generalized roles. Primarily preachers or priests having teaching and ritual functions, they also possess administrative and judicial roles. As well as officiating at services ecclesiastics are responsible for organizing the erection of prayer houses and keeping them in a good state of repair, writing letters making arrangements for visiting preachers, looking after the

---

[1] Welbourn, 1961, p. 197.

THE OFFICIALS OF THE SECTS

63

finances of the group in their care, judging disputes between their subordinates and ensuring that the moral conduct of the members conforms to the rules of the church or sect. Ecclesiastics are ranked in a hierarchy, but those at all levels have ritual, administrative, and judicial functions, though the particular functions of officials at each level in the hierarchy are clearly different.

Specialist secretaries or clerks specifically concerned with administration are found at the headquarters of some sects; often they are not members of the ecclesiastical hierarchy but rather paid employees. In the Faithful Church of Christ in 1959–60 the secretary was not even a member of the sect, but of a nearby Church of Scotland congregation.

The pattern of the ecclesiastical hierarchy is similar in all the sects and in the Church of Scotland, though the titles of the offices vary, sometimes between congregations of one sect. All the titles are English, but they are frequently treated grammatically as Chinyanja words. In the following description of the offices I use the titles which are most frequently used in the Faithful Church of Christ, but indicate alternatives which are used in some other congregations.

The leaders of all the African sects, except the Providence Industrial Mission, are their founders; subordinate to them are hierarchies of four offices held by men and one held by women. In some very small African sects with only one or two congregations this male hierarchy is truncated.

Deaconesses

Women officials are known as deaconesses in most sects and as sisters in others. The title 'Deaconess' or 'Sister' is not added to their personal name, nor is it used as a term of address. They do not usually wear any special uniform, although in a few sects, notably the Seventh-day Baptists, some have white robes which they wear at baptisms. They are not paid officials, but are chosen by the local minister and members of the congregation. Each congregation usually has between two and five deaconesses; one is often the minister's wife. A deaconess accompanies each girl at her baptism, leading her to the edge of the water, holding a towel and dry clothing for her, and going with her into the bush when she goes to change her dress. Under the leadership of the minister's wife, they may prepare food for preachers and other visitors to the congregation. They play little formal part in services, although they may take the lead in selecting hymns to be sung before the service actually starts. Occasionally one

64   SECTARIANISM IN SOUTHERN NYASALAND

or more may sit at the table at the front of the prayer house together with the minister and elders. On one occasion, at a service of the African Church Crucified Mission, a deaconess was called upon to make an extempore prayer after the sermon, but this is not a general practice in other sects. There is little prestige attached to the office, frequently members of a congregation have only a vague idea of who its deaconesses are. No ritual surrounds the appointment.

Deacons

The lowest level in the male hierarchy is the deacon, known sometimes as a monitor. The local minister, advised by members of his congregation, appoints three to five of their number as deacons. No ritual is involved in their appointment and they wear no insignia of office. The deacon's duties include acting as guardians to men and boys being baptized, and carrying out many of the functions of traditional burial partners at the funerals of Christians.[2] They may also act as informal counsellors to the local ministers in judging disputes which come before him. Sometimes they assist, and occasionally take the place of, the *unkhoswe*[3] in maintaining harmonious relations between Christian spouses, though this is usually left to elders and local ministers. Deacons are expected to play a leading part in the corporate activities of the congregation, repairing the prayer house, plastering the house of a member of the congregation, or helping to cultivate a sick member's gardens. They are appointed largely on the basis of their personality and the length of time they have been Christians; they are reliable members of the congregation who are known to adhere fairly well to its rules (those who do not are demoted). They do not need educational qualifications nor do they undergo any training. The deacon's office carries little prestige and the duties are thought by some to be rather menial. It is, however, the first rung on the ladder of the ecclesiastical hiearchy and many deacons hope to rise higher.

Elders

The office of elder is the next level in the ecclesiastical hierarchy.

---

[2] See p. 60.

[3] The *unkhoswe* are male matrilineal relatives of the spouses, usually their brothers or mothers' brothers, who meet together if there are any disputes between the man and wife or if either of them or their children fall sick. They should be present if a dispute, or a request for a divorce, is taken to the Native Authority Court. A fuller description of their role is given on pp. 112–13.

THE OFFICIALS OF THE SECTS

65

There is no female equivalent to this office. Each congregation usually has two or three elders, though some smaller ones may have only one. Elders are in sole charge of a few small outlying congregations belonging to White sects, but this does not occur in African sects, who are more ready to appoint ministers. They are appointed by the minister in charge of the congregation in consultation with its members and the appointment ratified by a senior official of the sect. Elders are appointed to the congregation of which they are already members, not, like ministers, appointed from one congregation to serve in another. No ritual surrounds their appointment, neither do they wear any insignia of office and they are not paid. Some prestige attaches to the office of elder, however, particularly in some of the larger White sects and the Church of Scotland, where they may also earn the respect of people who are not members of the congregation—they are people able to read the Bible and often to preach from it. These two latter qualities, together with the person's character, are the main criteria by which elders are selected from the ranks of deacons. In the White sects, and the Church of Scotland in particular, the office of elder is frequently held by school teachers employed in the local mission school and by others who have become clerks, veterinary assistants, storekeepers, etc., and thus become familiar with some of the techniques of a Western way of life. This seems to be more true of Mlanje than Chapananga's area, the inhabitants of Mlanje generally having a higher standard of education. In these cases elders are those who have done well according to the new system of values in Southern Nyasaland and their appointment to office is a recognition of this.

Elders play an important part in the congregation's worship and during services they sit at the table facing the remainder of the congregation (as distinct from deacons, who sit with the general body of the congregation). They often read the passages of scripture, make extempore prayers and may on occasion preach a sermon. They, more frequently than deacons, assist the minister in judging disputes between members of the congregation and infringements of the sect's rules.

The office of elder is the highest level in the hierarchies of the Church of Scotland, White sects and one African Sect—the Providence Industrial Mission—to which a person can rise without formal education beyond the Sub-Standard level and specific training.

66 SECTARIANISM IN SOUTHERN NYASALAND

The local minister

The local minister (in some congregations known as a pastor or evangelist) is normally in charge of a single congregation and responsible to a minister who supervises a number of congregations. He conducts its services and administers its affairs. He may be addressed as 'Pastor' and this term may be added to his personal name to form a title thus—'Pastor Business', though in other congregations the terms 'Mr.' or 'Ce'[4] are more frequently used. A local minister does not wear any insignia of office.

Local ministers in the Church of Scotland, White sects, and the Providence Industrial Mission normally receive a period of training varying between six months and two years at the mission headquarters or a special school. Here they receive Bible instruction and are taught the doctrines of the sect. Local ministers must be literate in Chinyanja, but many have little knowledge of English. In the Church of Scotland and White sects, some, though not all, local ministers have previously been elders, but some are recruited from ordinary members of the congregation. In the African sects, however, almost all the local ministers have previously been elders, either in the sects in which they now hold office or else in others. This is the normal pattern of recruitment in African sects,[5] but not necessarily in the White ones, where, if a member of the congregation has sufficient education and wants to become a minister, he may be accepted for training without having first held a lower office.

Senior officials of the sect, be it African or White, appoint the local minister to the congregation. He is not necessarily appointed to the congregation of which he was a member before his appointment, but most African ministers are appointed to such congregations or to new ones being established nearby. The appointment of a local minister involves certain rituals. I witnessed this in the Faithful Church of Christ when Muwati was appointed a local minister in a service at Chaima village in Zomba District to serve in a nearby congregation.

After the end of the weekly Sunday service, which was attended by members of several nearby congregations of the Faithful Church of Christ, Severe, the head of the sect, explained that the appointment was to be made. Muwati then came from his seat among the elders and stood at the front of the congregation facing them. Severe asked him, in a voice audible

---

[4] A Chinyanja term denoting mild respect to a man—usually translated as 'Mr.'
[5] For a fuller description of this point, see below pp. 83–4.

THE OFFICIALS OF THE SECTS

67

to the whole congregation, if he agreed to keep the laws of the Faithful Church of Christ. He replied that he did agree. Three other ministers then joined Severe and the four of them stood in a circle around Muwati, each placing a hand on Muwati's head and praying silently. While they were still in this position the congregation and the ministers together repeated the Lord's Prayer and the service was completed. Muwati then shook hands with the ministers and Severe presented him with a Bible and a hymnbook.

The local minister officiates at most services in his congregation, assisted by an elder who reads the passages of scripture, makes some of the prayers and occasionally preaches. He is responsible for preparing candidates for baptism, and in sects where an examination is held, for examining them. Usually, however, the baptismal service is taken by a more senior official of the sect (often a White missionary in the White sects), who asks the candidates a few questions before the service to ensure that they have been taught the rudiments of Christianity adequately. In the baptism services I attended, both in White and African sects, the local minister himself immersed the candidates in the river while the more senior official conducted the service from the bank. Local ministers, too, are responsible for conducting the funeral services of members of their congregation who die.

Local ministers should ensure that members of their congregations adhere to the rules of the sect and attempt to settle disputes between members. Together with their congregation they may hear disputes in the same way as village headmen hear disputes between their villagers. Such disputes may be brought to the minister even when one of the disputing parties is not a Christian.[6]

In the Church of Scotland and most White sects local ministers receive a small stipend, which, by its regularity, enables them to live at a slightly higher standard than the majority of their congregation, who are largely dependent upon subsistence cultivation with a cash crop of tobacco or cotton for their livelihood. Some are also provided with bicycles enabling them to visit members of their congregation more easily, and to attend meetings at the sect headquarters or at other congregations. In the African sects very few local ministers receive a stipend. A few are paid in the Faithful Church of Christ, as this sect receives financial assistance from the United States, but most

---

[6] See below, p. 119.

68 SECTARIANISM IN SOUTHERN NYASALAND

African sects lack the resources with which to pay their local ministers. Those local ministers in African or White sects who do receive a stipend are not entirely dependent upon it for their livelihood. Being a local minister is not a full-time occupation—where local ministers in the Church of Scotland and most White sects are appointed to a congregation in a village where they do not already possess rights over garden land, they are usually allocated such rights by the village headman. This appears to be the case much less frequently in African sects. In these sects local ministers are usually in charge of congregations in villages where they already possess rights over land, or they continue to live in such a village while they are in charge of a congregation in another village nearby. This is partly due to the reluctance of many headmen to grant rights over land to local ministers in African sects who come from other villages, and partly the result of the process by which African sect congregations are formed.

The position of a local minister, particularly in the Church of Scotland or a White sect, is one of prestige in the changing system of values in southern Nyasaland, it is a position which is recognized even by non-Christians. It is this which causes the struggle for leadership described below (pp. 81–94), and which underlies the process of sectarianism in Mlanje.

The minister

Supervising and overseeing the work of local ministers or pastors are ministers, usually responsible for several congregations, in some cases twelve or more. Ministers in the Church of Scotland and some larger White sects derive considerable prestige from their position and are known, not only to members of the congregations under them, but also to non-Christians and members of other churches and sects in the area. Generally they have received at least a Standard Six and in some cases a Standard Seven education and consequently have a good working knowledge of English. In African sects, on the other hand, only a few ministers, except those in the Providence Industrial Mission have received more than a Standard Two education, and they, unlike their counterparts in the White sects, have received no special training for their office. Likewise ministers in African sects do not have the same status outside the sect as the minister in the White sect or the Church of Scotland.

In some sects, and particularly in the Church of Scotland, ministers

THE OFFICIALS OF THE SECTS 69

are addressed and referred to as 'Reverend' and sometimes wear a clerical collar and black stock as a sign of office. This is not the case in all sects, some White missionaries do not style themselves 'Reverend' and many do not wear clerical collars. African ministers in these sects and sects which have seceded from them usually follow their example.

In addition to supervising the work of local ministers in a certain area, ministers are usually in charge of a large congregation of their own. This congregation tends to be a local centre of the church or sect and often has a school attached to it. The minister may also teach in the school and be partly responsible for its supervision.

Ministers in the Church of Scotland and White sects, some in the Faithful Church of Christ, and a few in other African sects are paid. Many ministers in the Church of Scotland and the White sects are appointed to areas where they have no rights over garden land either by their own or their wife's descent. They spend more time on affairs connected with their office than local ministers; often they are away from their own congregations for several days at a time, travelling around other congregations preaching and baptizing and attending meetings. As a result the minister is more dependent upon his stipend and upon gifts from the congregations for his livelihood than the local minister.

Ministers of a church or sect together form a synod responsible for administration and certain policy decisions.[7] In the Church of Scotland there are regional synods composed of ministers in a particular area who send representatives to the central synod of the Church of Central Africa (Presbyterian). In smaller localized African sects local ministers may also be members of the synod.

The founder or head of the sect

In the White missions the chairman or president of the synod is the White missionary or superintendent; in the African sects it is the founder or head of the sect. The place of some White missionaries in the Church of Scotland has now been taken by Africans as part of the programme of Africanization of the Church of Central Africa (Presbyterian). Such Africans are educated at least up to a Cambridge Junior Certificate level and may be regarded as operating very largely within a White system of values. In some instances Africans and

---

[7] A meeting of such a synod is described on p. 120.

70 SECTARIANISM IN SOUTHERN NYASALAND

Whites hold equal positions on the staff of Church of Scotland mission stations.

White missionaries are seconded from the Church of Scotland in the United Kingdom to work with the Church of Central Africa (Presbyterian) in Nyasaland; this latter is now an autonomous body, however. In most White sects White missionaries are responsible to parent organizations overseas—usually churches or sects, though White missionaries in the Nyasa Mission and the Zambesi Mission are responsible bodies created specifically for the purpose of missionary work in Nyasaland. The Mikalongwe Mission is an exception. This is autonomous: its founder was a White missionary originally sent by the Baptist Industrial Mission to work on their mission station, but who subsequently seceded and founded his own mission.

The *de facto* position of the White missionary is essentially similar in all the White Protestant missions. The superior status of the White *qua* White, which is characteristic of Southern Africa, is more significant in relations between missionary and congregation than any differences between one mission and another. The pattern of White superordination is so much a part of life in Southern Africa that it is difficult for the missionary either to dissociate himself or be dissociated from this attitude. This White superordination has not, however, been in itself a major cause of sectarianism in Southern Nyasaland.

Our main concern in this section is, however, with the organization and leaders of African sects. These leaders attempt to operate, as far as possible, in accordance with their conception of a White system of values.[8] None regard themselves or are regarded in any way as prophets or charismatic leaders. The degree to which the head of the African sect is successful in gaining and keeping a following is largely correlated with his understanding of the White value system and the extent to which he has apparently been able to adopt a way of life which conforms with the stereotype of Western culture. The most successful sect leader, in terms of the size of the sect, is Dr. Daniel Malekebu, the leader of the Providence Industrial Mission, the oldest of the African sects. Dr. Malekebu qualified at an American university and spent nearly twenty years in the United States. The next largest African sect is the Faithful Church of Christ, founded much more recently in 1949 by E. C. Severe. This sect had some thirty

---

[8] With the exception, it would appear, of Peter Nyambo, the founder and leader of the Ethiopian Church.

THE OFFICIALS OF THE SECTS 71

congregations in 1959; Severe has a Standard Eight education and has also spent a few months in the United States. At the other end of the scale, the Reverend Rogers, the leader of the *Kagulu ka Nkhosa*, only received a sub-standard education, and although the sect has been founded over twenty-five years it has expanded little, and has still only one congregation. Rogers lives in a typically traditional wattle and daub house with little furniture, and his standard of living is regarded as being below that of a local minister in a White sect.

Dr. Malekebu appears to have been appointed to his position as head of the P.I.M. partly, at least, as a result of his familiarity with a Western way of life. He was a member of the sect shortly after its foundation, but went to the United States in 1907 and to an American university. The sect was disbanded by the Government in 1915 when Chilembwe was put to death as a result of the Chilembwe Rising. Dr. Malekebu was out of Nyasaland for many years before and after the rising and was allowed by the Government to re-start the sect in 1926.

In all the other African sects the leader, in 1959, was the founder. With the exception of John Chilembwe, none of the founders of African sects with which I had contact in Mlanje had died. All the leaders of these sects have previously been officials in other sects. Severe, the head of the Faithful Church of Christ, was previously an elder and schoolteacher in the African Church of Christ. Rogers, the head of the *Kagulu ka Nkhosa*, was an elder, and Maloya of the Sent of the Holy Ghost Church was a local minister in the Zambesi Mission. The head of the African Nyasa Church, Phombeya, was previously a minister in the Nyasa Mission. Chateka, the head of one of the Seventh-day Baptist sects, was previously a minister in Alexander Makwinja's Seventh-day Baptist sect, and Makwinja was assistant to an American Seventh-day Baptist minister. Nakule, the head of the African United Baptist Church, was a minister in the Providence Industrial Mission. The heads of the Sons of God and the African Church of Christ were previously ministers in the British Churches of Christ.

No ritual is involved in the appointment of the head of a sect— those at present holding the position have merely seceded from another sect and set themselves up as heads of autonomous groups.

Some sect leaders style themselves 'Reverend'—others do not; in this they appear to follow the example of the White missions from which they have seceded. None of them wear clerical collars or any other insignia of office; they have nothing to compare with the famous

72   SECTARIANISM IN SOUTHERN NYASALAND

black cloak of Isaiah Shembe, the Nazarite Church leader in Zululand.[9]

Most heads of sects have gardens on which they are, partly at least, dependent for food. Some receive an additional income from their religious activities, either in the form of a salary from a sect in the United States or gifts from their followers—but in most cases this amount is very small or non-existent. Usually the founders of sects establish their headquarters in a village where they already possess rights over garden land. They may then attempt to attract a following from among their relatives and friends and be given permission by the village headman to build a prayer house. Severe, for instance, was an elder in an African Church of Christ congregation in Zomba District, but when he started the Faithful Church of Christ he returned to Wendewende village, where his father was a *nyakwawa* (assistant village headman) and received land for the erection of a prayer house. Appendix A shows the extent to which he was successful in persuading his relatives nearby to become members of his sect. Severe now has a very considerable amount of garden land surrounding his headquarters, and as his sect is supported financially from the United States he is able to employ labourers to cultivate it. Maloya, head of the Sent of the Holy Ghost Church, established the headquarters of his sect in the village where his wife's matrilineal kin had rights over land; the headman of the village where he had been a pastor for the Zambesi Mission refused him permission to erect another prayer house in his village. He now receives American financial support, but still does some cultivation himself. Several founders of sects are sons of the chiefs or village headmen, and this may have helped them to gain permission to erect the headquarters of their sects. Rogers, the head of the *Kagulu ka Nkhosa*, on the other hand, has his headquarters in the village where he was already an elder in the Zambesi Mission and where he already held rights over land. He, with his wife's help, cultivates his own gardens.

The prestige or status attached to being the head of an African sect varies considerably—it appears—according to its size. Dr. Malekebu, head of the Providence Industrial Mission, is very well known throughout Southern Nyasaland, and is highly respected by many who are not members of his sect. Severe, the head of the Faithful Church of Christ, is known throughout much of Mlanje and Zomba Districts

---

[9] See Sundkler, 1961, p. 113.

THE OFFICIALS OF THE SECTS

73

—people going in the direction of his headquarters, whether members of his sect or not, frequently state that they are going *kwa Severe*. A few, but not many, inhabitants of Blantyre/Limbe that I met knew of Severe, whose headquarters are some twenty-five miles from the township; all knew of Dr. Malekebu.[10] At the other end of the scale, the leaders of sects with only a few congregations are not generally known much beyond the catchment area from which their followers are drawn. They do not appear to be respected or enjoy prestige except in the eyes of their congregations; others take little notice of them.

In many religious associations outside Nyasaland the death of the founder has confronted his following with the problem of finding a successor acceptable to all. In many cases the resulting crisis has led to sectarianism. The early history of Islam, for example, was faced with such a crisis on the death of Mohammed, and several sects in South Africa have also split on this issue. This crisis has not yet occurred in any of the African sects with which I had contact, but as there is likely to be competition for his position, particularly in the larger sects, the death of a founder may well be the focal point of further sectarianism. Phombeya, the head of the African Nyasa Church, suggested that one of his ministers, possibly his son, would succeed him. His son's claim would not, however, be based on descent, but on the fact that he was already a minister. Sect leaders and ministers do not express the idea that the position of the head of the sect should be inherited on the basis of descent as it has been in some South African sects. [11]

The Ethiopian Church

The nativistic Ethiopian Church has a similar hierarchy of ministers, local ministers, and minor officials. My knowledge of this sect is unfortunately largely drawn from contacts with only two congregations newly formed in N. A. Nazombe's area in April 1959 after the 'Declaration of a State of Emergency' in Nyasaland. In neither congregation had a local minister been formally appointed at that time.

---

[10] Prestige, of course, is not necessarily synonymous with being well known. Severe, in fact, was thought by some outsiders to be something of a charlatan— nevertheless he was pleased by the fact that he was well known in the area, and several outsiders brought problems to him.

[11] Shembe's son, for instance, took over the Nazarite Church on his father's death in 1935. (Sundkler, op. cit., pp. 117–21.)

S.S.N.–F

74 SECTARIANISM IN SOUTHERN NYASALAND

Those in charge of the congregations were expecting to be appointed local ministers in the near future. Each had started the congregation in his own village and invited ministers and local ministers from other Ethiopian congregations to come and preach. Village headman Ntepha, an important Nguru headman, was in charge of one congregation, and Kwatula, a *nyakwawa* in the nearby village of Phodogoma was in charge of the other. Neither of them had previously been Christians in any other sect (in this way they were distinguished from most local ministers in other African sects.) Both hold positions in the traditional political hierarchy, as does Peter Nyambo, the head of the sect, who is a village headman in the Ncheu District. The possible significance of this is discussed in the next chapter.

The Roman Catholic hierarchy

None of the African sects with which I had contact in Nyasaland had an ecclesiastical structure modelled on the Roman Catholic hierarchy.

The Catholic hierarchy of lay officials and priests is a rigid one; the gap between these groups is bridged only by ordination after a period of training lasting many years and following the acquisition of a Standard Eight or higher education. African priests in Southern Nyasaland are considerably outnumbered by White ones. Catholic priests are ordained by bishops, which the Catholic Church alone in Mlanje possesses (except for the African Methodist Episcopal Church, with which I had no contact). The administrative structure of the Catholic Church is pyramidal and 'segmentary'; the ultimate authority is the Pope and the head of the segment in Nyasaland the bishop —a single person and not a synod. This pyramidal structure is based upon the doctrine of Apostolic Succession by which ritual authority is handed down through bishops to priests. The dividing line between priests and laity is thus not only in terms of their training but also in their ritual and secular authority. The distinction in the Church of Scotland and the sects in Nyasaland is much less rigid.

The ordination of the Roman Catholic priest involves a considerable amount of ritual and ceremonial.

The outlying congregations of the Catholic Church are under the immediate care of a lay official. These acolytes have not the same degree of autonomy as the minister or pastor in the sects. As pointed out in Chapter IV, Mass is the central service of the Catholic Church and can only be celebrated by priests; other services are taken by the

THE OFFICIALS OF THE SECTS

catechist in the prayer house belonging to the local congregation but their form is laid down in a service book and there are no extempore prayers, and although there is a sermon it is not the central feature of the service.

The most significant differences, for a study of sectarianism, between the Roman Catholic hierarchy and those of the sects are thus, in the first place the priests' possession of ritual authority, secondly the much smaller amount of autonomy granted to minor officials in the Catholic Church, and thirdly their autocratic bishops who perform some of the functions of the democratic synods. These factors militate against sectarianism in the Roman Catholic hierarchy.

VII

THE ROLE OF SECT OFFICIALS IN NYASALAND SOCIAL LIFE

PAUW, writing of the Tswana on the Taung Reserve in South Africa, has stated: 'The opportunities for leadership in the churches now make up for the loss of such opportunities in the political and administrative sphere.' This is equally true of Mlanje. To possess a following in Southern Nyasaland, as in many parts of Central Africa, is to acquire prestige, and indeed traditionally in the absence of any form of storable wealth, it seems to have been almost the only way of doing so. In the traditional social structure status was a combination of achievement and ascription, but the changes that have taken place during the present century have curtailed the opportunities for achieving status according to traditional values. The churches and sects, however, now provide new opportunities for the achievement of status. Some of the values and processes associated with the traditional political system are now found in the ecclesiastical hierarchy, and a description of this system, and the changes which have taken place in it, is necessary for an understanding of sectarianism in Southern Nyasaland.

It is just possible that at one time, before the arrival of the Yao, the Nyanja were united under a paramount chief. Livingstone refers to a Chief Undi ruling over the area from the River Luangwa to Lake Shirwa, but whose 'empire' had already been broken up long before his own arrival in the area in 1860.[1] It seems certain, however, that if such an empire existed its effects were not felt in Mlanje or Chapananga's area during the period immediately prior to the arrival of the Whites.

Werner also refers to a 'Paramount Chief Lundu' who was ruling the area from the Shire river to Lake Shirwa and the River Ruo in 1861.[2] A matrilineal descendant of Lundu still rules over a small area of the Shire Valley but has no power over any other chiefs either in the valley or in the Shire Highlands. It also seems doubtful if he had such power at the time of the arrival of the Whites.

At the end of the nineteenth century the areas that are now Chi-

---

[1] Livingstone, 1865, p. 256.   [2] Werner, 1908, p. 256.

SECT OFFICIALS IN NYASALAND SOCIAL LIFE 77

kwawa and Mlanje Districts were ruled by a number of petty independent and autonomous chiefs. The charter for chieftaincy was the 'principle of primacy'.[3] The first headman to establish himself in an area and effectively assert his independence of other chiefs was recognized as chief—*mwini dziko*—the 'owner' of the country. The position was subsequently inherited matrilineally. The present chief Nazombe in Mlanje District, for instance, is a matrilineal descendant of a son of a former chief Mkumba. The first Nazombe[4] left his father's chieftaincy on the western side of Mlanje mountain and founded a new chieftaincy to the east. The present chief states that he was appointed by the Government because he is a descendant of the first person to settle in the country. A similar system seems to have operated among the immigrant Nguru; Ntepha for instance, the Nguru headman who first introduced the Ethiopian Church into Nazombe's area, considers that the Government should recognize him as a chief because one of his predecessors was the first Nguru to settle in the country.

A second and associated feature of the traditional political organization was the characteristic process of binary fission. This occurred at all levels of the political hierarchy and also in the *mbumba* (localized matrilineage), and is still sometimes a means of resolving conflict in the latter.

Several chieftaincies seem to have been formed by the secession of powerful village headmen, and at least one of those now recognized by the Government in Mlanje has been formed in this way since the arrival of the first missionaries. The first chief Nkanda, a Yao, was a village headman under Chief Mpama, whose successor still rules over an area near Chiradzulu mountain in the Shire Highlands. Nkanda rebelled against Mpama and went to live at the foot of Mlanje mountain some thirty miles away, where he set himself up as a chief.[5]

It seems that there was little a chief could do, short of using physical force if he could muster it, to prevent a powerful headman from doing this. Personal qualities of leadership were essential for a chief to acquire or maintain his position; without such qualities he

---

[3] Mitchell, 1956, p. 61.

[4] Chiefs and village headmen take the names of their predecessors and the system of 'perpetual kinship' operates for chiefs and headmen, i.e. they succeed to the genealogical position of their predecessors—thus Chief Nazombe is a 'perpetual' son of Chief Mkumba.

[5] MacDonald, 1882, Vol. I, p. 32.

78 SECTARIANISM IN SOUTHERN NYASALAND

was likely to find that part of his chieftaincy had seceded under a powerful headman. The chief had scant formal executive machinery to help him maintain his position. Frequently no kinship ties existed between the chief and a large proportion of his following. Some of the qualities of leadership required of a chief seem to have been his ability to settle disputes fairly and to appoint village headmen who would support him and who in turn would be supported by their villagers. The chief was also the intermediary between his subjects and the spirits of his deceased predecessors who were responsible for the welfare of the land; in particular it was his duty to make supplications to the spirit of the first chief of the area for rain. Success in this probably strengthened his position—failure weakened it.

The office of chief was hereditary in a matrilineal line. Ideally the eldest son of the eldest sister of a deceased chief succeeded, but if he was considered unsuitable another relative took his place.

Thus before the White administrators arrived the areas that are now Mlanje and Chikwawa Districts were ruled by a number of petty autonomous chiefs, each with little formal executive machinery and largely dependent upon personal qualities of leadership to prevent secessions in their chieftaincies. These chiefs seem to have had less than 10,000 subjects each.

These chieftaincies were composed of villages each under a village headman. Villages usually consisted of two or three *mbumba* (matrilineages) linked either matrilineally or patrilaterally, the patrilaterally linked *mbumba* being composed of matrilineal descendants of the wife of the headman or his predecessor who had married virilocally.[6] The actual size of the village varied according to a number of factors, not the least important being the personality, or qualities of leadership, possessed by the headman. A popular headman would have been likely to retain a larger following than an unpopular one. The village headman was normally the *mwini mbumba*[7] of the dominant *mbumba*.

---

[6] It is likely that in the traditional political organization Cluster H of Wendewende village, described in the Appendix, would have been an autonomous village. Mitchell has described in detail the composition of Machinga Yao villages in the Fort Jameson District (Mitchell, 1956, Chapters V and VI). Fort Jameson has been subject to far less immigration from Portuguese East Africa during the present century than Mlanje has, and the villages there seem to resemble more closely the traditional structure of Southern Nyasaland villages than those in Mlanje.

[7] The head of the *mbumba*—unlike most men the *mwini mbumba* marries virilocally in order to look after the *mbumba*. There was, and often still is, competition between brothers and occasionally between matrilateral parallel cousins for this position.

SECT OFFICIALS IN NYASALAND SOCIAL LIFE   79

The dominant *mbumba* consisted of matrilineal descendants of the first person to establish a settlement in the area and to be recognized by the chief as a headman. The chief granted an aspiring headman land for huts and gardens and the headman gave the chief a small gift of beer or maize at the time of the first harvest after the village was established. The first headman of a village thus depended upon support from matrilineal kin willing to go with him to establish a new village—and upon a grant of land and recognition from a chief. Subsequently the headmanship became hereditary in the matrilineal line in the same way as the chieftaincy—i.e. the eldest son of the eldest sister was the ideal heir, but he might be passed over and another matrilineal relative take his place if he was considered unsuitable.

The headman was responsible for allocating land to nuclear families in his village and for keeping law and order in it. Each headman had an open space (*bwalo*) near his house where he sat, accompanied by villagers, to hear disputes. Essentially the headman seems to have been an arbitrator, and if he failed to settle a dispute the parties involved could take it to the chief.[8] The settlement of disputes seems to have been an important aspect of the headman's duties and skill at reconciliation was recognized as one of the qualities necessary in the successful headman.

The headman also had ritual functions. His predecessors, after death, maintained an interest in the welfare of the village, and the headman was responsible for making offerings to their spirits. He interpreted the omens when selecting a new village site. Many were also given the right to hold initiation ceremonies by the chief.

Village headmen were ranked according to a number of criteria— by the 'principle of primacy'—i.e. the earliest headmen and their successors in a chieftaincy were considered senior. These usually possessed the right to hold initiation ceremonies—a further mark of seniority. They were also ranked on the basis of the size of their village, often coincident with ranking on the 'principle of primacy', but not always so. These methods of ranking did not, however, lead to the creation of any rigid hierarchy of political offices. The system was characterized rather by its fluidity and the continual competition for followers.

As a result of this competition villages were subject to fission in the same way as chieftaincies. A *mwini mbumba* wishing to become a

---

[8] Johnston, 1897, p. 468.

80   SECTARIANISM IN SOUTHERN NYASALAND

headman could go off and found a new village if he could find sufficient people to support him. Typically the parent village split into its constituent *mbumba* and the patrilaterally linked *mbumba* moved off and started a new village—the *mwini mbumba* becoming the new headman. I recorded a number of examples of this having taken place in the past in Mlanje and such secessions have taken place more recently in Chapananga's area. Mitchell describes the process in detail for the Machinga Yao.[9] Generally a chief was only too willing to recognize an aspiring headman and give him permission to start a village of his own. Chiefs themselves were in competition with other chiefs for followers and an aspiring headman bringing potential subjects increased their following. If the chief of the area in which an aspiring headman was already living would not recognize him, it was likely that an adjacent chief would offer him land.

Any sanctions which a chief or headman could use were thus considerably reduced by the possibility of secession from his village or chieftaincy. A chief or headman attempting to force his will on unwilling followers was likely to find that many had left him—and to lose followers was to lose prestige.

The assessment of prestige in terms of followers and the consequent competition for their allegiance, and the lack of a rigid hierarchy of offcials or a paramount chief were associated, at a time when the population density was lower than it is today, with the process of binary fission in the political organization. New political units completely independent of those from which they seceded were constantly being created. Conflicts were resolved not by revolution or rebellion but by the simple process of secession, a process through which those aspiring to political office could attempt to satisfy their ambitions.

There are several striking parallels between the process of sectarianism in the ecclesiastical organization of Mlanje and this process of fission in the traditional political organization.

The ecclesiastical hierarchy is the focus of competition for office. The local minister's congregation is his following and he derives prestige from its size as the headman derived prestige from the size of his village. African sects offer opportunities for those lacking education to acquire an office in an ecclesiastical hierarchy. This, I suggest, is the major factor in the formation of simple secessionist sects in Mlanje. Many informants, inhabitants of the area, interpret them in

---

[9] Mitchell, 1956, Chapter 8.

SECT OFFICIALS IN NYASALAND SOCIAL LIFE 81

these terms. One White missionary suggested they were 'symptomatic of the African disease of *"mafumu onse"* (all chiefs)'.

The existence of this struggle for ecclesiastical office is frequently recognized by members of the sects themselves. Severe, the leader of the Faithful Church of Christ, told me that he always had to watch his senior ministers, i.e. those immediately subordinate to him, since they were the people who were jealous of his position and liable to start a new sect, taking away his congregations.[10]

All the African sects in Mlanje with which I had contact, except the Ethiopian Church, had been formed by secession. All the founders had previously been officials in other sects either White or African. The sect official's secession and foundation of a new sect is a similar process to the traditional one where the village headman seceded and founded a new chieftaincy. Both assert their complete independence from the parent body and become completely autonomous, both usually draw the nucleus of their followers from the parent group, but subsequently attract new-comers. In both cases the actual point of fission is marked by a conflict between the new leader and the one to whom he was previously subordinate. As Marwick has demonstrated for the adjacent and culturally similar Cewa, witchcraft accusations were associated with points of conflict in the political organization and with fission.[11] In at least one case similar accusations of witchcraft were associated with the foundation of an African sect. Phombeya, the founder of the African Nyasa Church, was previously a minister in the Nyasa Mission. At that time he was accused of witchcraft by his wife's brother, a teacher in the same mission. Phombeya denied the accusation and brought a case against the accuser at the Native Authority Court. The accusations continued, however, and some members of the congregation supported the teacher. Phombeya then left the Nyasa Mission and started his own sect with the support of other members of his congregation. Similarly a number of congregations belonging to Alexander Makwinja's Seventh-day Baptist sect were said by local informants (who were not members) to be bad because they were full of witchcraft. Members were said to use witchcraft against each other, as they all wanted to become pastors or ministers.

---

[10] This has also been recognized by leaders of African sects in Zululand—Sundkler quotes the following passage from the constitution of the National Swazi Native Apostolic Church of Africa: 'No minister leaving this church shall form a branch of it; he had better join another church' (1961, p. 146).

[11] Marwick, 1952.

82 SECTARIANISM IN SOUTHERN NYASALAND

Like the traditional chief, the founder of an African sect has few sanctions he can employ to maintain his position and is thus largely dependent on his own personality.[12] Again, like the traditional chief, the African sect leader may attempt to draw part of the nucleus of his following from his matrilineal relatives if he is a *mwini mbumba*. Appendix A shows the extent to which Severe has done this. On the other hand, unlike the traditional chief, the African sect leader is involved in a Western system of values and his success appears partly to be linked with his understanding and ability to manipulate the techniques of a Western bureaucracy. A few sect leaders have control of money coming from the United States and they can redistribute this in a way which strengthens their own position.

The office of local minister or pastor exhibits similarities with the traditional headman's office, and the process of forming new congregations in African sects is in some ways parallel to the traditional process of forming new villages. Many local ministers in African sects have previously been elders or deacons in another sect or in the Church of Scotland. On joining an African sect they may bring part, sometimes the larger part, of the congregation in which they were previously minor officials with them. This group forms the nucleus of a new congregation over which the dissenting elder or deacon is appointed as local minister. The leader of an African sect is generally only too willing to accept the elder with a following who is aspiring to be a pastor; this extends his own following in the same way that a *mwini mbumba* aspiring to be a headman was able to extend the following of an adjacent chief. There are many examples of African sect congregations having been formed in this way. At Chaima village, for instance, in N. A. Mwambo's area in the Zomba District, Gresham Chimenya was an elder in the Sons of God. He had a disagreement with the local minister, who was supported by the head of the sect; he then asked to become a member of the Faithful Church of Christ, was accepted and brought almost the entire congregation of the Sons of God with him. Very soon he was appointed a local minister and a new prayer house erected about a hundred yards from the one belonging to the Sons of God. Chimenya and other members of the congregation state that they left the Sons of God because they had no

---

[12] I once asked Severe to what he attributed his success in founding and maintaining the Faithful Church of Christ when other Africans had had much less success. He told me: 'When I was in America I read a book called *How to Make Friends and Influence People*, and that has helped me a lot'!

SECT OFFICIALS IN NYASALAND SOCIAL LIFE 83

school. On the other hand, the Faithful Church of Christ has only one school at its headquarters some forty miles away and no one from Chaima attends it.

In the Faithful Church of Christ there are sixteen local ministers and eight ministers (all of whom have previously been local ministers in the sect). Ten of this total of twenty-four were previously elders in another sect or in the Church of Scotland, five were previously deacons and seven were previously members, but not officials, in these bodies. Only two of the twenty-four had not previously been members of other churches or sects; on the other hand, none had previously been ministers or local ministers outside the Faithful Church of Christ. Thus most local ministers in the Faithful Church of Christ, i.e. fifteen out of twenty-four, had previously been officials in other sects. The largest category is those who have previously been elders (the highest level in the hierarchy where the official is not in charge of a congregation of his own, and the highest level in the White missions to which a person can rise without receiving education and special training).

Some local ministers have been officials in a number of religious associations. Michael Chinga, for instance, a local minister in the Faithful Church of Christ, was first a member of the Roman Catholic Church, from which he was excommunicated for divorcing his wife, and became a member of the Providence Industrial Mission, where he subsequently became an elder. Here he was alleged to have embezzled funds belonging to the congregation, and so he left and became a member of the African Church of Christ, where he was accepted as an elder on his admission. After some time the minister in the African Church of Christ wanted to demote him, so he transferred his allegiance to the Faithful Church of Christ, where he was again accepted as an elder and was later appointed a local minister.

In the White missions local ministers are appointed by senior officials on the basis of their educational qualifications, the assessment made of them while they are attending a training course, their ability as preachers, and their understanding and adherence to a Christian/Western system of values. In the African sect the local minister frequently has little or no formal education; he must be able to read and interpret the Bible, to preach and be seen to adhere to some extent at least to a Christian/Western system of values, but he is appointed by the head of the sect mainly on his ability to acquire and maintain a following. The elder who aspires to have a congregation of his own

84   SECTARIANISM IN SOUTHERN NYASALAND

can often do so in the African sect if he can find sufficient followers, in the same way that the *mwini mbumba* who aspired to having a village of his own could do so in the traditional political system.

Although most functions of the local minister are quite different from those of the traditional headman, some are similar. Both have religious duties, the headman making offerings to his ancestors for the welfare of the village and the local minister leading prayers for the welfare of the congregation. More significant however, is the fact that both act as arbitrators in disputes, and today some disputes which would traditionally have been heard by the village headman are now heard by the local minister. Neither possesses the power to enforce a settlement. The sanctions possessed by the traditional headman were weak—villagers unwilling to obey him could leave; similarly the sanctions possessed by the local minister are weak—it is even easier to leave a congregation than to leave a village, no new houses have to be built and no new gardens have to be dug. Both officials are frequently judged by their ability as arbitrators in disputes.

In some African sects outside Nyasaland sect leaders have made an apparently conscious attempt to operate in a similar way to traditional political leaders.[13] This has happened less in Nyasaland, where officials in the ecclesiastical hierarchy have deliberately modelled themselves on their counterparts in the White Protestant missions rather than on traditional political officials. They have not adopted the titles of traditional chiefs; the similarities between them are based rather upon the assessment of prestige in terms of the number of followers and the similarities of systems of autonomous, independent, and loosely structured groups whose officials are competing for followers.

Today the ecclesiastical organization provides a means of acquiring followers for those unable to do so in other spheres. The African sects provide such opportunities for those unqualified to rise in the White mission hierarchies. What changes have taken place in the traditional political organization to prevent the achievement of status in that sphere today?

Two main sets of factors have intervened to change the traditional political system to its present form. First the establishment of the British administration, and secondly, the large-scale immigration from

---

[13] E.g. Duckworth, 1957, describes how the leader of a Nigerian religious community is surrounded by some of the circumstances of a Yoruba chief.

SECT OFFICIALS IN NYASALAND SOCIAL LIFE 85

Portuguese East Africa which has characterized the demographic development of Southern Nyasaland during the present century.

When the British administration was established in Nyasaland at the end of the last century it pursued a policy of 'direct rule', relying largely on a recruited police force to implement its authority. The District Administration (Natives) Ordinance passed in 1912 was a step in the development of the present system of indirect rule. Although the Ordinance was not applied in its entirety to Mlanje until 1928 (owing to difficulties in areas alienated to Whites), the general principles laid down seem to have been applied earlier. The aims of this Ordinance are clear from the following passage from the Government's Annual Report for 1911–12; 'The decay in the power of native chiefs and the tendency all over the Protectorate to the splitting up of villages into small family groups continues. . . . It becomes increasingly clear that some paid native authorities are required who shall be responsible to the District Resident for the good order and administration of their villages or areas.'[14]

The Ordinance provided that 'each district or sub-district was divided into a number of administrative sections, each under the charge of a principal headman as conditions rendered necessary. . . . Each administrative section was divided on similar principles into village areas (groups or villages), each in charge of a village headman.'[15]

The criteria used in selecting the principal and village headmen are not clear, but it seems that those who were previously recognized by the people as chiefs were appointed principal headmen and the more important of the traditional headmen were recognized by the administration.[16] It is clear, however, that not all the traditional headmen were officially recognized and that the administrative villages were frequently composed of more than one traditional village.

The office of principal headman has now been abolished, but the village headmen remain—their position being very similar to that laid down in the 1912 Ordinance.

In 1933 the 'Native Authority Ordinance' and the 'Native Courts Ordinance' were passed implementing the policy of 'indirect rule' in Nyasaland. Chiefs were appointed Native Authorities[17] and given the

---

[14] Quoted by Murray, 1932, p. 129.
[15] Ibid.
[16] Mitchell, 1949, p. 143.
[17] The Native Authority is officially the chief and his councillors (see North, 1961), but the title 'Native Authority' is commonly applied to the chief himself.

power to inflict certain punishments of fines and short terms of imprisonment, to make laws (subject to the approval of the District Commissioner) and to raise money for a Native Treasury. Courts were built and clerks employed and the chief became, as Native Authority, the local head of an administrative bureaucracy.

By no means all those chiefs who have been recognized as principal headmen were appointed Native Authorities. In N. A. Nazombe's area, for instance, there were previously four principal headmen. Again the basis on which Native Authorities were selected from the ranks of principal headmen is not clear, but it appears that the successors of the earliest six (or so) chiefs in each administrative district were chosen.

In both Mlanje and Chikwawa districts there are six Native Authorities responsible to the District Commissioner. There has been no attempt to create a senior or 'paramount' chief. Chiefs receive a salary totalling about £40 per month, enabling them to live at a much higher standard than the majority of their subjects.

At his court the Native Authority hears cases involving breaches of Government regulations and certain breaches of 'native law and custom', and he is empowered to inflict punishment, or, as is more frequently the case, to order compensation to be paid. At the court are offices for the payment of tax and the issue of licences for dogs, beer brewing, bicycles, trading, etc. It is also usually the local distribution centre for mail and a centre of employment for clerks, messengers, dispensers, agricultural assistants, and other officials.

As well as carrying out the duties of a Government official the Native Authority also carries out some of the functions of the traditional chief. In N. A. Nazombe's area in Mlanje these two roles have been separated by mutual agreement between the Native Authority and his mother's brother, who retains the functions of the traditional *mwini dziko*. The fact that the Native Authority is known by the traditional name of the chieftaincy, while the *mwini dziko* is known by his own personal name, reflects the relative importance attached to the two roles in current values.

To a lesser extent the village headman, too, is now an official in the bureaucratic hierarchy. Informants use the term '*mfumu*' for a headman recognized by the administration and '*nyakwawa*' for the head of a component section of a village who would traditionally have been an independent headman. English-speaking informants often refer to the *nyakwawa* as an assistant village headman. The more significant

SECT OFFICIALS IN NYASALAND SOCIAL LIFE 87

unit in the daily life of the inhabitants of the area is the unit under the administration's headman—i.e. the village. Asked where he comes from a man almost invariably gives the name of the village headman and not the *nyakwawa*. It is the village headman's name which appears on his bicycle licence, his tax receipt, and other documents associated with the administration. It is the village headman not the *nyakwawa* who must hear a dispute before it can be taken to the Native Authority court and must be consulted before a labour migrant may leave the country. The village headman is involved in all the paraphernalia of a Western type of bureaucracy—the *nyakwawa* is not—it is he who is regarded as having followers and thus prestige rather than the *nyakwawa*.

The importance of the village and its headman *vis-à-vis* the *nyakwawa* is reflected in the title of the headquarters of the Faithful Church of Christ. These headquarters are situated in a large village, Wendewende, containing some 430 taxpayers (male adults) and in a section of the village some distance from the headman's houses and courtyard. The *nyakwawa* of this section was Severe's father, himself a member of the Faithful Church of Christ before his death. The village headman, Wendewende, is a Moslem. The official title and address of the sect is, however,

> Wendewende Mission,
> P. O. Box 562,
> Limbe.

It is not merely a question of postal convenience, as the address is a P.O. box number.

The duties of a village headman fall into three broad categories, ritual, administrative, and judicial. His ritual role is now of limited importance—many village headmen are Christians, offerings are only occasionally made to the spirits of deceased headmen, and only a small proportion of adolescents are now initiated (the right to hold initiation ceremonies was previously the privilege of certain headmen).

The headman is responsible for ensuring that Government regulations are kept in his village, particularly those concerning payment of tax, sanitation, clearing of paths, etc. He also allocates land to elementary families living in the village and gives permission for immigrants to settle within its boundaries.

Each headman has an open space (*bwalo*) where he hears disputes involving members of his village. This was a traditional function of a

88 SECTARIANISM IN SOUTHERN NYASALAND

headman, but I have not come across any examples of a *nyakwawa* holding such a court except where he had been instructed to do so by a headman in his absence. The headman's role in such disputes is still that of a mediator; he has no power to enforce a settlement on unwilling parties, but all cases taken to the Native Authority court should previously have been heard by the village headman and he may be called as a witness. Most of the cases coming before the headman are disputes between spouses or affinal relatives or involve fighting or bad debts.

The village headman receives a small payment from the Government for helping to ensure that taxes are paid, but the amount is insufficient to differentiate his living standards from those of the villagers under him. If a beer drink is being held in his village, he may receive a pot of beer, but this will depend upon his popularity.

As bureaucratic officials in the administration's hierarchy, the village headman and the Native Authority are in a more powerful position than the traditional political officials. Where previously the chief could do little with disobedient subjects he now can, and does, employ sanctions backed by the administration and has an executive force of messengers to ensure that his orders are carried out. Likewise the village headman is in a stronger position. On more than one occasion I have heard a village headman haranguing villagers with threats of taking them to the chief and reporting them to the District Commissioner—apparently with some effect.

The position of Native Authority carries with it a great deal of prestige, and so to a lesser extent does the office of a village headman recognized by the administration; the position of *nyakwawa* carries little. These bureaucratic offices in the administration's hierarchy are still the focus of competition—but it is no longer possible for all those aspiring to positions of leadership to succeed in this sphere. The whole of the province is divided into Native Authority areas and there are no opportunities for creating new ones. Under the present system only a matrilineal relative of an existing Native Authority has the possibility of becoming a Native Authority. In cases where a Native Authority has been deposed by the administration for incompetence, inefficiency or seditious activity he has been replaced, not by one of his powerful village headmen, but by a matrilineal relative. Native Authorities are now appointed on the basis of descent, although the administration does appoint the candidate from within a narrow range of matrilineal kin which it considers will be most suitable for

SECT OFFICIALS IN NYASALAND SOCIAL LIFE   89

the post. The Native Authority is thus in a much stronger position than the traditional chief; not only has he the support of the Government but it is not possible for him to find that half of his chieftaincy has seceded under a powerful headman. If he is unable to maintain his position he may be removed, but this will be by the Government, and the crucial point is that he is unlikely to be replaced by a headman aspiring for the position.

The same is broadly true at the level of the village headman. The Government is reluctant to recognize more headmen—believing that too many are not in the interests of efficient administration. This is particularly true in Mlanje, where there is now no land available for the creation of new villages. This leads us to the second factor responsible for changes in the political structure.

The traditional political system depended upon a relatively low population density and the possibility of expansion into empty or relatively unoccupied areas. In the Southern Province as a whole the density of population in 1945[18] was 82 per square mile, in Mlanje it was 138 and in Chikwawa 31. These are very high densities indeed for rural districts in Central Africa. The density in Mlanje is particularly high, and moreover a considerable part of the district consists of uninhabited mountain and so the density in the settled part of the district is much higher than the figure quoted. The density in Chikwawa, on the other hand, while high for rural Central Africa, is very much lower than in Mlanje—here there is still land available for new settlements and certainly in Chapananga's area these were being created in 1959 and it was yet possible, though admittedly difficult, for an aspiring headman eventually to gain Government recognition.

The high density is due to immigration from Portuguese East Africa as well as a rapid rate of natural increase resulting from improved medical and other services.

Table III, which has been compiled from the Census Reports for 1931 and 1945, shows the increase in population during the intercensal period. The increase in the total population of Mlanje represents 59 per cent of the 1931 total compared with a figure of 28 per cent for Nyasaland as a whole. The increase of Nguru was greatest of all (63 per cent), so that by 1945 71 per cent of the total population were

---

[18] This is the last year for which detailed census figures are available. Official estimates suggest that between 1945 and 1957 there was an increase of some 29 per cent in the total population. There is no reason to suppose that the increase in Mlanje was less than the national average.

S.S.N.–G

90   SECTARIANISM IN SOUTHERN NYASALAND

Nguru—that is 71 per cent of the population of Mlanje were immigrants who had arrived in the Protectorate since the beginning of the century—or the descendants of such immigrants. This situation was commented upon in the Census Report for 1945: 'The increase in the Lomwe (Nguru) of 144,000 is significant for it represents an increase of 61 per cent during the intercensal period (1931–45) as compared with 95 per cent for the decennial period 1928–31. The Nguru invasion which took place in 1921 was commented upon in the 1931 report, where the inference was drawn that much of the increase in population was due to immigration from Portuguese East Africa. The 1945 figures indicate that immigration has at least slowed down, although considerable numbers must have entered the Protectorate

Table III

POPULATION INCREASE 1931–45

Mlanje		Yao	Nguru	Nyanja	Total
Mlanje	1931	8,618	92,736	32,411	134,431
	1945	11,684	150,644	45,190	209,522
Increase		3,066	57,908	12,779	75,091
% of 1931		35%	63%	40%	59%
		Nyanja	Nguru	Cikunda	Total
Chikwawa	1931	23,036	600	10,781	35,892
	1945	28,609	4,270	23,477	59,664
Increase		5,573	3,670	12,696	23,772
% of 1931		22%	612%	118%	65%
			Nguru		Total
S. Province	1931		235,636		757,541
	1945		373,371		1,003,610
Increase			137,735		246,069
% of 1931			59%		32%
Nyasaland	1931				1,599,888
	1945				2,044,707
Increase					444,819
% of 1931					28%

SECT OFFICIALS IN NYASALAND SOCIAL LIFE 91

since 1931. As was to be expected, the districts most affected are Mlanje and Cholo, where the increase in this tribe is recorded as 99,000 out of a total of 144,000.'[19] The Government has made efforts to curtail this immigration—but it appears to have met with only limited success.

In Chikwawa, while the increase in population during the same period was proportionately larger (65 per cent) than in Mlanje, this represented an increase in density of only 12·5 per square mile. In this district, too, the increase in immigrants (in this case Cikunda) is most marked—188 per cent above the 1931 figure.

Thus the present political system, although ostensibly based on the traditional system, differs considerably from it. The traditional avenue to power and prestige is now blocked except for those succeeding, on the basis of descent, to an already existing office. The boundaries of the political units in the administrative structure are stable, but this stability is due to the presence of the superior power of the colonial administration and is not a reflection of the indigenous structure. Fission no longer takes place in the political structure in Mlanje and the aspirant for office must attempt to satisfy his ambition in another sphere of social life.

That he does this in the African sects is suggested both by the fact that these sects are replicas of the White sects from which they seceded—i.e. they have not seceded on the basis of doctrinal differences—and also by the fact that they appear to have a much higher ratio of officials to members of the congregation than the White missions.[20] Unfortunately I have no figures to demonstrate this 'overstaffing'—due largely to the difficulty of assessing the size of congregations,[21] but many services I attended in African sects were also attended by a minister and local minister and several elders and deacons even where the total congregation was less than forty. I did not encounter this plethora of officials in the White missions.

---

[19] Census Report for Nyasaland, 1945, Government Printer, Zomba.

[20] I also gained the impression in the field that the African sect hierarchies contained a high proportion of sons of chiefs and headmen. Unfortunately this is only an impression gained from a large number of examples and I lack the statistical material to demonstrate it. If this is the case, it may be significant in that it was frequently the sons of chiefs and headmen who traditionally moved off and started new political units. It may also be the case, however, that sons of chiefs and headmen have found it easier to get a site on which to establish a congregation within their village than people unrelated to the headmen have done.

[21] See p. 23.

92 SECTARIANISM IN SOUTHERN NYASALAND

Sometimes African sect officials do, in fact, attempt to usurp the village headman's duties. Severe, for instance, attempted to by-pass the village headman and take three court cases, including a dispute over land, straight to the Sub-Native Authority,[22] but this official refused to hear them and ordered that they should be referred back to the village headman. I have heard one case accepted by Native Authority Nazombe's court where it had previously been before a minister in the Church of Scotland instead a village headman. This was an application for divorce, and the minister was well known and highly respected in the chieftaincy.

The Ethiopian Church

The significance of the Ethiopian Church hierarchy in relation to the traditional political hierarchy appears rather different from that of the simple secessionist sects. The Ethiopian congregations which were being formed in N. A. Nazombe's area in 1959 were not being formed by secession as I have described it for the Faithful Church of Christ at Chaima. Neither of the leaders of these congregations had previously been an official of another congregation—in fact, both were previously pagans. I think it may be significant that in both cases they were men who held a political office which was more important in the traditional system of values than it was in 1959: Kwatula was a *nyakwawa* in the village of Phodogoma and Ntepha was a village headman. The Ethiopian Church, particularly in the case of Ntepha, appears to have provided an opportunity for someone with status in the traditional system of values, status which had gone unrecognized in establishing the present political hierarchy, to acquire a position in a hierarchy which reflected partly traditional values and partly new Western ones.

Ntepha invited the Ethiopian Church to his village shortly after a court case at N. A. Nazombe's court at which he had been the main defendant. I attended the court case and have described it in detail elsewhere.[23] I outline here only the salient features relevant to the present discussion.

In early District Books for Mlanje, Ntepha's predecessors are referred to as 'chief' and later as principal headmen, and today

---

[22] A councillor from the court of the Native Authority who holds a court in an outlying part of the Chieftaincy.

[23] Wishlade, 1961.

SECT OFFICIALS IN NYASALAND SOCIAL LIFE 93

Ntepha is generally regarded as the successor to the first Nguru chief in the area.

About a month after the 'State of Emergency' was declared in Nyasaland in March 1959, Nazombe summoned a number of Nguru headmen, including Ntepha, to his court. He asked them if they had attended a meeting about a month previously at the village of one of their number—Msikita. One headman replied that he had heard there was to be a meeting there and then admitted it was Ntepha himself who had told him about it. One of Chirapula's[24] councillors then said that he had been at Msikita's village on the day in question and seen a dance organized by Ntepha, who had sacrificed a goat and chickens to the spirits of his predecessors, asking for rain. Nazombe at this stage became angry, saying that Ntepha had no right to organize this dance, that it was Chirapula's privilege as *mwini dziko*. This was an insult to Chirapula and to himself as Native Authority. Ntepha replied that he and his predecessors had been performing the dance for a long time.

Another witness told the court that after the dance had been performed those involved held a meeting at which a local official of the African National Congress was in the chair. The witness said that at this meeting it was stated that the *mwini dziko* should be Ntepha, and that Msikita, his sister's son (a perpetual relationship), should be Native Authority—he had been a school teacher and so knew English and the ways of the Whites. Nazombe emphasized that he was the Native Authority because he had been appointed by the Government.

Four of the headmen, including Msikita and Ntepha, then had their tax registers taken from them by the court clerk on Nazombe's instructions. They were told to return the following week with two councillors from their villages, and Nazombe said he would appoint a 'committee' [*sic*] to do the work of the Government in the village until he had told the District Commissioner of what had taken place. In fact, the District Commissioner was never informed and the tax registers were returned to the headmen about three months later.

I discussed the case afterwards with Ntepha, when he again emphasized his position as the successor of the first chief in his particular area. About a fortnight after the case he, together with a pastor in the Ethiopian Church, invited me to attend the first service of the Ethiopian Church in his village. Up to this time there had been no

---

[24] Chirapula was Nazombe's mother's brother and the *mwini dziko* of the area (see p. 77).

94   SECTARIANISM IN SOUTHERN NYASALAND

Ethiopian congregations in Nazombe's area and Nazombe had declared himself opposed to the sect. Ntepha invited the Ethiopian ministers to start the congregation in his village, and the service was held in the open space outside his house after his wife had prepared food for the visitors. During the service, which was conducted by two visiting ministers, Ntepha was called upon to stress the importance of making offerings to ancestral spirits. After the service a visiting minister suggested that Ntepha should write down the names of those present (they numbered about thirty, but did not include Msikita or any other of the headmen involved in the court case) and continue to hold services in his village, attempting to build up a congregation. This he did.

It does seem here that Ntepha was trying to use his position as the successor to important predecessors as a basis for acquiring a following in the Ethiopian Church. This following would be drawn from a wider area than his own village and recognize the importance of his matrilineage. The Government had failed to recognize his status when they appointed Nazombe as Native Authority—the Ethiopian Church did recognize it.

Unfortunately I lack the material to assess how far this is true of other Ethiopian congregations, except to point out that Kwatula appears to be in a similar position lower down the traditional hierarchy. As a *nyakwawa* he held an office in the traditional hierarchy, but the position was not recognized by the Government, who had appointed Phodogoma headman over the area in which Kwatula lived. Clearly factors other than the struggle for office are involved in the formation of Ethiopian congregations—fundamental differences of doctrine, for example—but this struggle, which I have suggested is the mainspring of the formation of simple secessionist sect congregations, is not entirely lacking as a factor in the spread of the Ethiopian Church.

The Nyasaland African National Congress[25]

I have suggested that the simple secessionist African sects provide

---

[25] After its proscription in 1959 the Nyasaland African National Congress was subsequently re-formed as the Malawi Congress Party. Here I use the name by which it was known during my fieldwork. The study of Congress was not part of my fieldwork plans and to do so in the disturbed political situation of 1958/59 would have been impossible without alienating informants or the Government or both. My information about Congress is therefore largely based on second-hand sources.

SECT OFFICIALS IN NYASALAND SOCIAL LIFE   95

opportunities for the acquiring of status or office for those unable to do so in the administrative hierarchy. What other alternative offices are there? The Nyasaland African National Congress provided one possible alternative until it was proscribed in March 1959.

Congress was formed in 1944 as a convention of several associations concerned with African advancement and welfare (none of them appear to have been connected with African sects). When it was founded there was no single national grievance strongly binding all its members; this was provided in 1953 by the federation of Nyasaland with the Rhodesias. Congress declared itself opposed to the Federation and was associated with 'disturbances' in various parts of the country, including Mlanje, in 1953 and again in 1959. The official Commission of Enquiry set up to inquire into the 1959 'disturbances' suggested, however, that they were probably due to 'a general feeling of unrest rather than to anti-federation views'. It further stated that 'the Africans in these parts had grievances relating to the tenure of land and the disturbances had apparently a non-political source'.[26] Informants also suggested to me that some of the minor disturbances in February and March 1959 in Mlanje were only partly connected with the question of federation.

In these cases it appears that one possible factor was the conflict which I have described resulting from the application of the policy of indirect rule to the indigenous political organization of the area. Although no 'disturbance' arose from it, the meeting held at Msikita's village immediately after the performance of the rain ritual was attended by Congress members and a Congress official was in the chair. These people declared their support for Ntepha as *mwini dziko* and said that when Dr. Banda took over the country Msikita would be Native Authority. Nazombe, at his court, addressing village meetings and in conversation, repeatedly avowed his support for the Government and his disapproval of Congress activities. He was aware, and emphasized, that his power was the power of the Government. Congress gained the support of Ntepha, Msikita and others in the area, not primarily because of its campaign against the Federation, but owing to its general opposition to the Government and its representatives. The conflict between chief and powerful village headman, traditionally resolved by fission, appears to manifest itself in terms of a new institution—the Nationalist political party.

---

[26] *Report of the Nyasaland Commission of Enquiry*, 1959, para. 23.

96   SECTARIANISM IN SOUTHERN NYASALAND

In an adajcent chieftaincy the situation was similar but reversed. Here the Native Authority, Nkumba, was himself a supporter of Congress. Bwanaisa, one of his powerful village headmen, was attempting to undermine his position by currying favour with the Government. Bwanaisa met with a certain amount of success, but when Nkumba was deposed (in October 1959 after I had left the field) he was replaced by a matrilineal relative and not by Bwanaisa.

Between February and March 1959 a number of disturbances took place at Native Authority courts in Nyasaland. The *Report of the Commission of Enquiry* cites an example of such a disturbance. 'On 27th February the first shooting in the Southern Province occurred at the court of Chief Chigaru. The trouble was foreshadowed by an incident which took place at the court of another chief, Lundu. Some days before Chief Lundu had summoned a meeting of village head-men for February 21st. Several did not come, saying they had to attend a Congress meeting. So he summoned them to appear, pre-sumably for contempt, at his court on February 24th. They came with a crowd, threw down the summons with '*Kwaca*'[27] written across it, and said that he must not prosecute any more for breaches of agricul-tural rules.[28]

Lundu is a Nyanja chief in the Shire Valley in Chikwawa District and an acknowledged Government supporter. The situation here seems parallel to that existing in Nazombe's area.

It would be wrong to suggest that this kind of conflict was the only source of support for Congress. Clearly in the urban areas many other issues were involved, but in Nazombe's area at least it does appear to have been an important source of Congress support, although Con-gress was less powerful in this chieftaincy than in some other parts of the Southern Province.

Congress, like the African sects, is also modelled on a Western type bureaucracy. It has its central and local committees with chair-men, secretaries, treasurers, and other officials. It provides a hierarchy of offices in which an aspiring official can attempt to find a place and thus prestige.

There are, so far as I am aware, no formal links between Congress and any African sect, and I have no evidence to suggest that the pro-portion of active Congress members was higher in the African sects

---

[27] A Congress slogan which literally means 'dawn'.
[28] *Report of the Commission of Enquiry*, 1959, para. 133.

SECT OFFICIALS IN NYASALAND SOCIAL LIFE 97

than in the White ones.[29] It appears that the African sects and Congress may be alternative ways of acquiring an office. No ecclesiastical officials I met in African sects admitted also to being Congress officials.

This tentative hypothesis that in southern Nyasaland the African sects and Congress are alternative avenues of expression appears to be supported by the fact that the Ethiopian Church, in particular, expanded very rapidly after Congress had been proscribed. It was not, for instance, until after Congress had been banned and was unable to give Ntepha active support that he turned his attentions to the Ethiopian Church.

On the other hand, if they are alternative avenues of expression, Congress had not been subject to the fission that characterized the traditional political system and characterizes the African sects. One of the outstanding features, in fact, of the Nyasaland African National Congress (and its successor the Malawi Party) has been the united front which it has presented to the outside world. There are a number of possible explanations for this.

In the first place the unity of Congress at the local level in rural areas may not be so striking; it is possible that the local branches and committees are the focus of a struggle for office—this I do not know. Even at the national level the arrival of Dr. Banda from England in August 1958 seems to have been only just in time to prevent secessions in Congress from becoming apparent.

The structure of Congress is also very different from that of the traditional political structure or that of the sects. It is a rigid hierarchy firmly directed from the top—local officials do not have the same degree of autonomy and independence as either the traditional headman or the local minister. Congress is a single pyramidal structure—there is no series of similar structures in which it is possible for the ambitious to move from one to another in search of promotion. In Congress there is no precedent for fission: in the African sects, on the other hand, the fact that there were already several separate White missions operating in the same area provided the example for the formation of still more. The common opposition of all Congress members to the Federation may also have aided its unity. It may be that if it achieves the goal of the secession of Nyasaland from the Federation strong measures will have to be taken to maintain the

---

[29] Indeed, its closest links seem to be with the Church of Scotland.

98   SECTARIANISM IN SOUTHERN NYASALAND

unity of the party. Finally, Government officials and others have stated that Congress gained some of its support through a 'reign of terror'; if this is the case, and I have no first-hand evidence that it was so in 1959, it would also help to explain the absence of fission in this sphere.

The Roman Catholic Church hierarchy

The structure of the Roman Catholic Church is pyramidal with the Pope at the apex. Every other official in the Catholic hierarchy is subordinate to a higher official. Weber describes the Roman Catholic hierarchy as 'one of the examples of rather distinctly developed and quantitatively large bureaucracies'.[30] The distinctive feature of the Roman Catholic hierarchy *vis-à-vis* other ecclesiastical hierarchies in Southern Nyasaland is not, however, so much its bureaucratic characteristics—all the sects are to some extent bureaucratic—but the possession by its officials of, in Weber's terms, 'institutionalized charismatic authority'. According to the Catholic doctrine of Apostolic Succession a 'gift of grace' is imparted to the Catholic priest at his ordination. By this 'gift of grace'—or charisma—officials in the Catholic hierarchy possess supernatural authority. The priest possesses the ability to impose supernatural sanctions, an ability which he can and does exercise. Those, for instance, who do not attend confession and carry out the imposed penance are not allowed to receive the element at Mass. Excommunication from the Catholic Church commits a believer in its doctrines to the realm of the damned. The Catholic priest is clearly in a very different position from that of the official in the Protestant hierarchies. The Protestant minister does not possess institutionalized charisma,[31] he does not receive a 'gift of grace' on his appointment. The Protestant minister is not able to impose divine sanctions and the Protestant churches and sects in the area do not regard themselves as the one true church and the only source of salvation. Expulsion from a Protestant church or sect does not of itself commit a person to everlasting damnation; there are other churches he can join.

Catholics accept the Apostolic Succession as an unbroken chain of authority stretching back to Christ. The only way in which a priest can receive valid and effective ordination is through a Catholic bishop.

---

[30] Gerth and Mills, 1948, p. 204.

[31] He may possess personal charisma shown by his ability as a preacher—but this is not bestowed on him at his ordination.

SECT OFFICIALS IN NYASALAND SOCIAL LIFE 99

A person cannot appoint himself a Catholic priest, but he can appoint himself a Protestant minister without running counter to the main doctrinal tenets held by the Protestant missions operating in Mlanje. In the Protestant churches and sects, unlike the Catholic Church, no elaborate ritual surrounds the appointment of its officials and they are not regarded as part of an unbroken chain of authority. There are already many similar Protestant hierarchies and a person seceding from one of them can attempt to create a structural replica of the parent body from which he has seceded; this he cannot do in the Catholic Church.

African Catholic priests are some of the most highly educated and Westernized inhabitants of Southern Nyasaland. They are less influenced than most by traditional values and have a high status according to the new emerging values which have a high regard for education and the degree to which a person is acculturated. Those who have been ordained into the Catholic hierarchy would have little to gain in terms of status and prestige by seceding and attempting to form a sect of their own.

Catholic catechists and other lay officials, who are not ordained, do not possess charismatic authority but are appointed by priests on the basis of their education and moral standards. Catechists in charge of outlying congregations have far fewer opportunities for exercising qualities of leadership than local ministers in the Protestant churches and sects. They are not entitled to perform the main Catholic ritual— the Mass—this is the prerogative of priests. The form of service which the catechist leads is laid down in detail; there are no extempore prayers and the sermon plays a much smaller part in the service than in Protestant services. The catechist is usually more closely supervised than the local minister; the majority of the White missionaries in Southern Nyasaland are Catholics and they have many more mission stations than any Protestant mission. This enables priests to pay frequent visits to all their congregations and perhaps to heal any breaches in them before they may result in secession. The catechist consequently has much less independence and autonomy than his counterpart in the Protestant missions, and the similarities between his position and that of the traditional headman are much less marked. The catechist's congregation, unlike the local minister's, is not his following; he is regarded rather as the representative of the priests at the mission station than the leader of a local group. Thus although there is prestige attached to the office—it is less the result of having followers than showing oneself to be sufficiently educated and acculturated to be appointed to a position in a Western hierarchy. It is the prestige of the school teacher and the clerk—prestige in terms of the new emerging values rather than in terms of traditional ones.

To transfer from the Catholic Church to a Protestant sect involves basic changes of doctrine, and, which is perhaps more obvious to Africans in Southern Nyasaland, changes of ritual. To transfer from one Protestant sect to another does not involve such radical changes and may involve none at all. Some movement of individuals from the Catholic Church to others does take place in Southern Nyasaland, but the proportion of Catholics who change their allegiance is only a fraction of the proportion of Protestants who do so.

This does not mean that secessions resulting in the formation of new sects from the Roman Catholic Church have not occurred in Central Africa; they have.[32] But there are clearly characteristics of the Catholic Church which, while not entirely precluding the formation of African sects from among its ranks, do inhibit the development of the simple secessionist type of sect characteristic of Mlanje. I have suggested that these characteristics may be found in its rigid hierarchical structure based upon institutionalized charismatic authority.

---

[32] See, for instance, Taylor and Lehmann, 1960, pp. 106–8.

VIII

THE SECT AS A SOCIAL GROUP

CHURCHES and sects are voluntary associations recruited ostensibly on the basis of the common religious beliefs and experiences of their members. These beliefs are formulated in doctrine and expressed in ritual. In both doctrine and ritual, however, the simple secessionist sects in Mlanje differ little from the White missions from which they originated. Common religious beliefs and experiences are clearly thus not the only factors involved in determining a person's religious group. In the last chapter I suggested that the struggle for office was of prime importance as a factor in sectarianism in Mlanje. Leaders must have followers, however, and social factors also play a part in determining their religious affiliation.[1]

Sects and local grouping

One of the most obvious of these factors is residence. A person who changes his place of residence may be forced to change his religious affiliation, not as a result of any new religious experience, but simply because of the lack of a congregation belonging to his particular church or sect in the area into which he has moved. Christopher, for instance, who lived in Tombondera village in Chapananga's area, was a member of the Universities' Mission to Central Africa, an Anglican mission operating in the Central Province of Nyasaland, but when he moved to Tombondera he became a member of the Zambesi Mission, whose doctrine and ritual differ considerably from that of the Anglo-Catholic U.M.C.A.

Only the Roman Catholics and the Zambesi Mission have congregations in Chapananga's area. The settlement pattern here is nucleated and all Christians living in one settlement usually belong to a single congregation—the nearest one. This is partly because the density of population is lower than in Mlanje which, coupled with the pattern of settlement, means that congregations tend to be some distance apart, and partly the result of there being only two missions operating in the

---

[1] The beliefs and practices of the various churches and sects must also fulfil certain emotional or spiritual needs of their members. This aspect of them is, however, beyond the competence of the present writer.

102   SECTARIANISM IN SOUTHERN NYASALAND

area. This is not the case in Mlanje, where, although place of residence is significant in religious affiliation, it is as a limiting rather than as a determining factor. Here the majority of Christians are members of one of the nearby congregations, but a few travel to others some distance away.

Describing the peri-urban area of Blantyre/Limbe, Bettison has stated: 'In certain villages . . . it was clear that religious affiliation was of considerable weight in the delineation of cluster formations.'[2] In Mlanje the reverse is true; place of residence is normally determined by factors other than religion, but itself limits the choice of religious groups to which a person may belong. This limitation, however, generally applies only to the sects: Roman Catholic, and to a lesser extent Church of Scotland, prayer houses are so widely distributed throughout the district that almost every settlement is in easy reach of one.

Sects and kinship ties

Christian spouses usually belong to the same congregation and in some cases one or other spouse changes religious affiliation on marriage. As marriage is normally uxorilocal, it is usually the man who changes when he moves to his wife's village. Choice of a spouse is largely an individual matter in Southern Nyasaland, and in some instances, particularly in the case of Roman Catholics, the religious affiliation of a prospective partner has been one of the factors influencing the choice. In all the cases recorded in my censuses where a person had changed from one congregation to another after marriage their spouse had changed, too.

I recorded details of the religious affiliation of ninety-nine couples in Mlanje and Chapananga's area. In eighty cases both spouses were of the same religious affiliation—in fifty-five they were both Christians, and in twenty-five they were both pagan.[3] In fourteen cases the husband was pagan and the wife Christian, and in three cases the husband Christian and the wife pagan. These three included one woman who was a member of the Church of Scotland with her husband, but who left to brew beer, and one widow who had recently married a Christian widower, but was still living in the house erected

---

[2] Bettison, 1959, p. 58.

[3] This does not represent the proportions of Christians and pagans living in the area, as the sample is far from being representative—my introduction to some of the settlements involved was through African sect congregations.

THE SECT AS A SOCIAL GROUP

by her former husband. In only two cases did the husband and wife belong to different Christian denominations.

Unmarried children usually belong to the same religious group as their parents, but here the factor of education is important. Children of pagan parents may attend Christian schools and may be baptized or be attending baptism classes in the church or sect to which the school belongs. There are, moreover, more congregations than schools and Christian parents may send their children to schools belonging to other congregations if there is no school attached to their own denomination in the area. These children may then become members of the church or sect from which they received their schooling.

Matrilineages (*mbumba*) are more heterogeneous in their religious affiliation than elementary families. The *mbumba*, which is the only social group based upon descent, is not a residential group. The female members of the *mbumba* together with the *mwini mbumba* and unmarried males normally live in one residential cluster, but other men normally marry uxorilocally and are consequently dispersed in a number of clusters.[4] The women of the *mbumba*, that is a group of sisters and their daughters, frequently work together in an informal group, pounding maize and carrying out other domestic tasks. Periodically they are visited by their brothers who have married elsewhere. Affines living in the cluster are clearly distinguished from members of the *mbumba* and this is reflected in the use of the term *kamwini* (stranger) to address or refer to them.

Although it is the only descent group, the *mbumba* is not important as an economic unit. Land is allocated by village headmen to households rather than to *mbumba*. It is an important unit in the regulation of marriage, but this does not involve a transfer of wealth (except that in the case of a divorce compensation is almost inevitably demanded and the *mwini mbumba* is expected to help his female dependants to find this). The elementary family is a more important unit economically

---

[4] The boundaries of the *mbumba* are not always clearly defined; younger brothers of the *mwini mbumba* living in other villages may sometimes repudiate his authority and say that they are members of no *mbumba*. Marwick (1952b) states that the adjacent and culturally similar Cewa apply the term *mbumba* only to the female relatives of the *mwini mbumba* and use *mphwa-* for younger male relatives, but he also states that the *mbumba* consists of the dependent male and female relatives. The *mwini mbumba* has certain rights over and obligations towards dependent male relatives regardless of their place of residence, rights and obligations mainly concerning marriage. Here I use the term *mbumba* to include these male dependants.

104   SECTARIANISM IN SOUTHERN NYASALAND

than the *mbumba*: a returning labour migrant, for instance, is expected to give substantial presents to his wife; he may also give a small gift to the *mwini mbumba*, but he is more likely to give one to his father.

Traditionally the *mbumba* was an important ritual group. Indigenous religious activity was centred around the spirits of the matrilineage. It seems that no regular offerings were made, but that when a person dreamt that a particular spirit was complaining of neglect he told the *mwini mbumba*, who was the intermediary between the spirits and his dependants. The *mwini mbumba* then made an offering of flour or beer at the grave of the spirit who had been the object of the dream. Such offerings are made only infrequently today, even where the *mwini mbumba* is a pagan.

At traditional funerals members of the deceased's *mbumba*, his or her spouse, and perhaps the spouse's marriage witness shave their heads. Members of the *mbumba* should also ideally refrain from sexual intercourse until purification rites are performed about a month after the death. Some informants state that the *mwini mbumba* should end the period of prohibition by ritual intercourse with his wife. Christians generally do not participate in these rituals and the solidarity of the *mbumba* in this sphere has been weakened.

Today some members of the *mbumba* may be Christian while others are pagan, and in Mlanje Christian members of one *mbumba* may be members of different congregations. In cases where members of one *mbumba* are all members of one congregation this may be only indirectly a function of their common descent due rather to their co-residence in the same village and membership of the nearest congregation.

In some cases, however, where the *mwini mbumba* is a minister or important official in a church or sect, he may make efforts to include his *mbumba* in his following. Living in the same residential cluster as his kin, he is in a better position to do this than other men living with their affinal relatives. When Severe first established the Faithful Church of Christ he recruited some of his first members from his own *mbumba*, people who had previously been members of different churches and sects. Today, as can be seen from Appendix A, only one of his dependent matrilineal relatives is not a member of the Faithful Church of Christ. Both his brothers are officials at the headquarters of the sect: Antonio married his mother's brother's daughter's daughter, who was living in the same cluster as his own mother,

THE SECT AS A SOCIAL GROUP 105

and Bennet married uxorilocally into an unrelated but adjacent cluster some 300 yards away from Severe's house. Severe has not, however, been able to include members of a patrilaterally related *mbumba* (the core of the inhabitants of Cluster H in the Appendix) in his following.

Descent is thus only of limited significance in determining religious affiliation in Mlanje and Chapananga's area today.

Beyond the *mbumba* descent is the basis of membership of matrilineal clans. Traditionally burial partners responsible for funeral ritual were chosen on the basis of clan membership, but they are non-localized and non-corporate and important today only as exogamous categories.

The African sect's attraction for followers

In the last chapter I suggested that the simple secessionist sects provided opportunities for acquiring followers for those unable to do so in other fields of social activity. That this appears to be the mainspring of simple secession is supported by the high ratio of officials to other members. Leaders, however, must have followers and the sects must have some attractions for them, too.

In discussing the attractions of African sects it must be remembered that only a relatively small proportion of Christians belong to them. Out of 576 congregations in Mlanje only 133 belong to African sects, and these are generally smaller than those belonging to the White missions. Clearly we may assume that the African sects are generally less attractive than the White missions.

Membership of any church or sect in Southern Nyasaland appears to offer other attractions apart from the psychological or 'spiritual' satisfactions gained from taking part in religious ritual. Congregations are groups into which strangers ideally are accepted and within which they can make friends. Pauw indicates the importance of this for the Tswana on the Taung Reserve.[5] Southern Nyasaland has been characterized by large-scale immigration of small groups of matrilineally linked kin from Portuguese East Africa. As a result the population of Mlanje, in particular, is heterogeneous in origin. Villages consist of clusters of huts inhabited by completely unrelated matrilineages. The congregation provides a group larger than the matrilineage for co-operation in such things as house building and the cultivation of gardens. 'I was a Seventh-day Adventist, but I was

---

[5] Pauw, 1960, p. 67.

S.S.N.–H

106   SECTARIANISM IN SOUTHERN NYASALAND

expelled, and when I came to this village I was alone and so I joined the Faithful Church of Christ,' said one informant. This factor, however, appears of less importance in Southern Nyasaland than in the Taung Reserve. In Southern Nyasaland, where uxorilocal marriage is the norm, men are most frequently the strangers (*kamwini*) in a village, but in all the congregations I visited, except those of the Ethiopian Church,[6] more women than men attended the services.[7]

Their educational facilities are a major attraction of some churches and sects, particularly White missions. Primary education is almost entirely in the hands of religious groups, who run schools with the aid of Government grants. The majority of schools in Mlanje belong to the Roman Catholics and the Church of Scotland. Almost all the White sects, however, have a few schools which provide education up to Standard Three and in some cases beyond. There is, on the other hand, a great deal of variation in the attitude of various missions towards education. The Roman Catholics and the Church of Scotland regard it as a major part of their work, and at their mission stations are schools which provide teaching up to, and in a few cases beyond, Standard Six. At the other end of the scale a missionary in the Assemblies of God told me that they regard education as primarily the work of the Government, though they do provide a few schools with classes up to Standard Three.

Most African sects have no schools. The African Nyasa Church, however, has a school built with a Government subsidy and with qualified teachers paid with a Government grant, and the Providence Industrial Mission has several such schools. The Faithful Church of Christ has one school at its headquarters at Wendewende, providing classes up to Standard Three. This, however, is financed entirely from the sect's own funds; the Government rejected a request for a subsidy.

---

[6] The Ethiopian congregations had more men than women participating in their services and were unique in this respect. Wilson, noting a similar feature in two African sects among the Nyakyusa of Tanganyika, suggests that it may be due to their lack of prohibition on polygynous marriages. (Wilson, 1959, p. 190.) For further discussion on this point see below, pp. 115–16.

[7] The greater attraction of Christianity for women rather than men appears widespread, not only in Nyasaland but in many parts of the world, including the present-day western Europe. This seems unrelated to social structure except in so much as Christianity seems to appeal more to the subordinate members of the community, who in many societies are women.

THE SECT AS A SOCIAL GROUP 107

The failure of the African sects to provide schools makes them less attractive to potential followers than the White missions. This failure is partly due to the lack of funds; although the Government subsidizes schools some capital is still required to build them. District Education Committees, who are responsible for allocating funds, have, moreover, a large representation of White missionaries and are reputed by African sect leaders to be reluctant to grant them subsidies. It seems to be the case, however, that the African sects find it very difficult to recruit teachers sufficiently qualified to be eligible for a Government grant. On a number of occasions when Severe was visiting congregations of the Faithful Church of Christ he was asked by village headmen and others who were not members of the sect to provide schools in their villages. The reply was always that there was insufficient money available. There is a very strong desire for education in Southern Nyasaland and those sects possessing schools are at an advantage in the competition for members. Churches and sects provide schools, not only for the children of their own members but also for the children of pagans. In some cases schools may attract children of parents of another denomination. In Mbeza village in N. A. Nazombe's area, for instance, some members of the Church of Scotland send their children to the Assemblies of God school. This latter is situated near to the Church of Scotland school, but charges lower fees. The school an adolescent attends is often important in deciding the church or sect into which he is baptized.[8] All the sects and the Church of Scotland practise adult baptism which may take place after a few years' attendance at school.

The lack of tribal sentiment in Southern Nyasaland appears to be associated with the desire of Africans in this area to live as far as possible according to their conception of a White way of life. This lack of tribal sentiment is probably the result of a number of factors some of which were indicated in Chapter III. There is no political centralization, tribes are not political units. There is no economic differentiation leading to the development of a socio-economic class system based upon tribe which would tend to perpetuate a tribal sentiment; the immigrant Nguru, for instance, are not a class of immigrant labourers, they are not differentiated economically from the other peoples of the area. While missionaries have opposed pagan practices in general, they have not directed their opposition at the practices of

---

[8] See also Bettison, 1959, p. 52.

108   SECTARIANISM IN SOUTHERN NYASALAND

any one tribe and thus helped to foster its tribal identity.[9] None of the tribes in Southern Nyasaland have art forms or highly developed rituals by which they identify themselves. Even the nativism of the Ethiopian Church is not a desire to perpetuate the ritual of any particular tribe; in fact, its members are drawn from the immigrant Nguru and the aboriginal Nyanja, and the leader, Peter Nyambo, is Ngoni.

This desire of Africans to live as far as possible a White way of life leads to the caricature of Western institutions that has so often been described for other parts of Africa. In Southern Nyasaland this desire is expressed in many forms—Western-type dress, for instance, is almost universal among men and spectacles without glass are often worn. Some people use cutlery and most use mugs and cups. People enjoy sending and receiving letters on all possible occasions and using English when, in fact, the vernacular is much better understood. At a Western-type dance in Zomba, for instance, those present continually spoke English to each other despite the fact that no Whites were present (except myself) and the majority understood Chi-Nyanja more readily. Clearly many products of Western technology such as bicycles, radios, glass windows, etc., are adopted because they are useful and make life easier and more enjoyable, but not all the items of Western civilization adopted fall into this category—some are taken over just because they appear to be Western.

Christianity is associated with the West and this is one of its major attractions.[10] The outstanding feature of the simple secessionist sects in Mlanje is their attempt to copy as far as possible all the features of the White missions from which they originated. The White missions, on the other hand, are recognized as the genuine article and thus have a greater attraction in this respect than the simple secessionist sects.[11]

The caricature of a Western type of committee meeting, which took place at the headquarters of the Faithful Church of Christ and is described later in this chapter, illustrates the way in which the African sects attempt to copy the details of bureaucratic procedure. At one

---

[9] The intense opposition of missionaries in Kenya to Kikuyu female initiation ceremonies appears to have been a factor in maintaining tribal sentiment in this politically acephalous tribe.

[10] Islam, on the other hand, is not associated with the West and is thus less attractive in this respect. In spite of the fact that Islam was introduced into Nyasaland through the Arabs before Christianity, it has not expanded at anything like the same rate.

[11] cf. Pauw's statement that on the Taung Reserve 'Non-separatists feel that their churches are "just a bit more genuine" than the separatists.' (Pauw, op. cit., p. 109.)

THE SECT AS A SOCIAL GROUP

service in the Faithful Church of Christ the officiating minister conducted the service with a camera hanging from his neck: it was in a leather case which remained open throughout the service. A flash gun (without a bulb) was mounted on the top, although it was midday and the skies were clear. I failed to appreciate the full significance of this until some time later I attended a service at an outlying congregation of the Assemblies of God in N. A. Nazombe's area. The service on this occasion was conducted by a White American missionary who, as soon as he stepped from his Volkswagen, took photographs of the congregation to send to the parent body of the mission in the United States. At the same service in the Faithful Church of Christ, Severe's wife, Cecilia, brought with her a young baby and a brief-case. During the service when the baby began to cry she opened the brief-case and brought out a feeding-bottle full of milk and attempted to quieten the infant with it. She was unsuccessful and after several attempts resorted to the traditional method of feeding an infant, which met with instant success.

Many Christians, both in African and White sects, possess their own Bibles; many have a good knowledge of their contents and are able to quote chapter and verse to support a number of arguments. A popular form of informal discussion among Protestants is the quotation of passage after passage of scripture together with short commentaries. Those possessing Bibles proudly carry them to the services and when lessons are being read conscientiously follow them. One member of the Faithful Church of Christ equally conscientiously followed them in a battered copy of *Tom Brown's Schooldays*!

Some African sects not only copy the White ones as far as possible but have attempted to become affiliated with White American sects operating in other areas. The Sent of the Holy Ghost Church, for instance, founded in 1934, succeeded in 1956 in becoming affiliated with the Pentecostal Holiness Church with its mission headquarters in Lusaka. One of the ministers in the Faithful Church of Christ, who had seceded and was attempting to form a sect of his own, was seeking affiliation with another American sect—the Church of the Nazarene. Such affiliation has a double attraction—it enhances the status of the sect officials, who then become officials in a White hierarchy, and it provides financial support. The simple secessionist sects are not anti-White; on the contrary, they are often anxious for White support, and their officials are well aware that the most abundant source of this support is the United States.

Several informants who were not members of the Faithful Church of Christ attributed its success, no doubt at least part correctly, to the parcels of clothing which are sent over from the United States for its members. Such parcels are clearly a great attraction to potential members, and this is made evident by the conflicts which arise over their distribution.

So far the attractions of membership of a religious group have been weighted heavily in favour of the White missions, and indeed these missions do have a membership at least five times as large as that of the African sects. Nevertheless, membership of African sects does offer specific attractions. In the first place they accept members who have been expelled from other religious groups.

The African Church of Christ and the Church of God were, in fact, formed as a result of disagreements about this issue. They were formed by ministers who had been in charge of the Church of Christ in the absence of a White missionary after the Chilembwe Rising in 1915. When a missionary returned he refused to sanction the baptism of people who had been expelled from the Church of Scotland and so the two ministers left and started sects of their own.

Robson, a member of the Faithful Church of Christ, was formerly a Seventh-day Adventist who had been expelled for marrying a second wife. He joined the Faithful Church of Christ after having deserted his first wife. Severe emphasizes that monogamy is one of the rules of his sect, and stated that if Robson had married his second wife while he had been a member he would also have been expelled from the Faithful Church of Christ, but as the offence had been committed before he applied for membership he was admitted. In the same congregation as Robson are two men who state that they were expelled from the Church of Scotland for not paying church dues— so far they had not paid any in the Faithful Church of Christ either. White missionaries and members of their missions have suggested to me that a considerable proportion of the membership of African sects is composed of people expelled from mission congregations. There is some truth in this.

African sects accept new members who have been baptized in another sect by total immersion, without the need for another baptismal ritual.[12] Movement from one sect to another is thus easy. Joseph

---

[12] This does not apply to those baptized by a token sprinkling, as, for instance, in the Church of Scotland.

was an elder in the African Church of Christ who applied for membership of the Faithful Church of Christ, saying that he felt the minister in the African Church of Christ was neglecting to visit him as often as he should. He came to the minister in charge of the congregation at Matewere village in Zomba District, and after Sunday service was called to speak to the congregation. He explained his reasons for wanting to leave the African Church of Christ and asked to be admitted to the congregation. After he had finished speaking, the minister asked all those in the congregation who were willing to accept him to raise their hands. Almost all the congregation did so and Joseph thus became a member.

Out of a total of fifty-four members of the Faithful Church of Christ resident in two villages, Wendewende in Mlanje District and Chaima in Zomba District, thirty-five had previously been members of one other church or sect, eleven members of two others and one a member of three others. Only seven were pagans immediately before they joined the sect.[13] Clearly not all these people had been expelled from their previous congregations, but the Faithful Church of Christ obviously recruits many more of its followers by proselytization than by evangelization.

Members of churches and sects are expelled for such offences as divorce, polygyny, drunkenness or taking alcohol, or failure to pay church dues. Ecclesiastical officials have also been expelled for embezzling funds—two local ministers in the Faithful Church of Christ told me that they had previously been expelled from another sect for this reason.

Generally it appears that African sects are more reluctant to expel members than White missions. White missionaries are anxious to maintain the moral standards of their congregations and expulsion is the ultimate sanction they can employ to this end. It is a sanction which is not infrequently employed. The leaders of the African sects, particularly the smaller ones, seem more anxious to retain their following, and thus their status, and are consequently more reluctant to expel members. Expulsions from African sects do, however, occur when blatant delicts are committed. Chidothe, a local minister in the Faithful Church of Christ, was expelled for taking a second wife while his first was in hospital suffering from leprosy.

---

[13] On the other hand, in Tombondera village in Chapananga's area only two out of a total forty-seven Christians had been members of more than one church or sect and these had both changed their affiliation on a change of residence.

112 SECTARIANISM IN SOUTHERN NYASALAND

A major attraction of African sects is sometimes thought by Whites to be their repudiation of the Christian/Western marriage norms imposed by missionaries.[14]

The selection of a spouse in Southern Nyasaland is very much a matter of individual choice outside the exogamous matriclan. There is an expressed preference for marriage between cross-cousins (either matrilateral or patrilateral), particularly between classificatory cross-cousins. This does not run counter to the tenets of any of the White missions and the marriages of some of their members are between *suweni* (cross-cousins).

There is little ritual involved in the marriage of either pagans or Christians. A man wishing to marry a particular girl tells his *mwini mbumba*, who discusses it with the girl's *mwini mbumba*. If both are agreeable, the bridegroom goes to the bride's village with a few matrilineal relatives, taking a hoe and maybe a few other small gifts, though there is no large-scale transfer of wealth. The bride cooks a meal for the visitors, who then return to their own village. The bridegroom then builds a house for his bride and should not sleep with her until it is completed; if his own village is nearby he returns there at night, if not he sleeps in a *gowelo* (a small hut used for sleeping by two or three unmarried boys) in his bride's village. When the house is finished the couple move in with a short ceremony in which they are exhorted by a *phungu* (a councillor—usually an old woman living in the village) to inform their *mwini mbumba* if anything goes wrong between them. This aspect of marriage has not aroused the general opposition of White missionaries.

Marriage witnesses (*unkhoswe*) have a key role to play in the social organization of Southern Nyasaland. Each married person should have two witnesses—a senior one, who is normally the *mwini mbumba*, and a junior one who acts as a go-between and is normally a brother. The witnesses should be informed of any illness within the elementary family and of any disputes arising between the spouses. It is the duty of the senior witnesses to attempt to settle any such disputes and to attend any court cases resulting from them. Today some liaisons are

---

[14] An account, apparently of the Ethiopian Church in Southern Nyasaland stated: 'Thousands of Africans in Nyasaland are flocking to join a church designed exclusively for sinners and people who wish to continue sinning and which regards polygamists and adulterers as its most saintly members.' This passage occurred in an article entitled 'Sinners are Saints in "Do What You Like Church",' *Sunday Mail*, Salisbury (S. Rhodesia) on 19 February 1961.

THE SECT AS A SOCIAL GROUP 113

contracted between couples without having marriage witnesses.[15] In cases where such couples have come before N. A. Nazombe's court for a divorce and for compensation to be determined, the Native Authority has argued that such liaisons are not proper marriages and that consequently no compensation can be awarded. The recognition of marriage witnesses is crucial to marriage.

The role of the marriage witnesses is recognized by both White missions and African sects. Christians and pagans have marriage witnesses, and in some cases Christian spouses may have pagan witnesses or the witnesses may be members of different churches or sects. In disputes between Christian spouses officials of the congregation may attempt to arbitrate, but they do so with the co-operation or the knowledge of the witnesses even if the latter are pagans. Missionaries have not generally attempted to undermine the position of the marriage witness. They recognize his role in helping to stabilize marriages in an area where they are traditionally unstable.

Marriage establishes a series of rights and obligations between spouses, some of which are traditional while others are of recent origin and dependent upon the introduction of cash. Marriage does not give a man jural rights over his children; these remain with their mother's matrilineal kin. It does not give a man the right to remove his wife to his own village; marriage here is permanently uxorilocal. Disputes sometimes arise when a man becomes a *mwini mbumba*, *nyakwawa* or village headman and has to go and live with his own matrilineal kin, and I came across several instances where a man's return to his own village for this purpose had led to a divorce. Several village headmen I met had married Sena women from the Port Herald District, saying that this avoided such conflicts. The Sena appear to marry virilocally (though no adequate account of their social organization exists), and in the cases I recorded between £8 and £10 was given to the bride's kin on marriage. Where a man has a successful business and has built a good house, he, too, may try to persuade his wife to move to his village; this also leads to disputes. Makuta, a fairly successful fish trader who had a brick house with a corrugated-iron roof, had been married virilocally for about twelve months. His wife grew tired of living away from her kin and came with her marriage witness and her husband to Nazombe's court asking for a divorce. Nazombe refused to consider the case until Makuta's marriage witness

---

[15] This seems less common in the rural areas than it is in the town. (See Ngwane, 1959.)

114 SECTARIANISM IN SOUTHERN NYASALAND

also attended the court, which he did the following week. On this occasion Nazombe and his councillors said that this was a difficult case; it was the custom of the country that a man should build a house in his wife's village—but here the man had a very good house and a business in his own village. They told the girl and her marriage witness to think again, that they were being very stupid to want a divorce when she could live in a good house. The girl, however, was adamant and so they were divorced.

A man is expected to build a house and to provide his wife with money to clothe herself and her children. If he is away as a labour migrant he should send money back for her. The woman is expected to cook her husband's food, and to carry out part of the cultivation of gardens. A man has exclusive rights of sexual access to his wife. I witnessed several cases at N. A. Nazombe's court where a man wanted a divorce from his wife because she had committed adultery, and demanded compensation from the adulterer. I witnessed no cases where a woman was seeking a divorce from her husband on the grounds of his adultery. Conversations with informants revealed that this was regarded as a much less serious offence. From the Christian/Western point of view, however, adultery by either party in marriage is equally culpable and is generally grounds for expulsion from a mission. This view is shared by the simple secessionist sects.

Failure to fulfil the rights and obligations of marriage frequently leads to a request for a divorce. Traditionally a divorce was recognized by the mutual exchange of a chicken between the marriage witnesses of the husband and wife. Divorce was, and is, easy.[16] Conjugal separation without divorce is also common—but today most people who are separated demand compensation from the other partner—and this necessitates divorce. The payment of compensation can only be enforced by the Native Authority, with the result that a large proportion of all the cases heard in the Native Authority courts are divorce cases.[17] Both Christians and pagans come before the Native

---

[16] cf.Gluckman's hypothesis that divorce is rare and difficult in those societies organized on a system of marked father-right and frequent and easy to obtain in other types. (Gluckman, 1950, p. 190.) Marwick, commenting on the divorce rate among the adjacent and culturally similar Cewa, suggests that the conjugal and matrilineal ties conflict to the detriment of the conjugal ones. (Marwick, 1952b, p. 261.)

[17] Out of a total of fifty-seven cases which I attended at N. A. Nazombe's court in Mlanje thirty-six cases were divorce cases. In most of these failure to meet the obligations of a spouse were alleged, but in a few cases the spouses merely said that they were tired of each other.

THE SECT AS A SOCIAL GROUP

Authority seeking a divorce; unfortunately I have no data capable of revealing if divorce was more frequent among pagans than among Christians.

White missionaries are well aware of the instability of marriage in Southern Nyasaland. The Roman Catholics do not recognize divorce and N. A. Nazombe, himself a Roman Catholic, always asked those coming before him for a divorce if they were Christians, and if so to what denomination they belonged. He refused to hear cases involving Roman Catholics—telling them they should go to the priest instead. Protestants are less rigid in their attitude, tending to treat each case individually. Nevertheless they do expel those of their members who become divorced and are deemed by them to be culpable. This provides a source of recruitment to African sects. The simple secessionist sects themselves disapprove of divorce and attempt to reconcile the parties in the same way as the White sects. Here again the difference between the simple secessionists and the White sects lies not in their rules, but in the formers' general willingness to accept those expelled from other sects. When a dispute arises between Christian spouses that may lead to divorce the local minister and elders may call the congregation together and hold an informal court in an attempt to reconcile them. These meetings occur in both White missions and African sects.

All the missions and the simple secessionist sects enjoin monogamy; none will countenance polygyny.[18] On the other hand, although some pagans practise polygyny, many pagan male informants state that they have no desire for more than one wife, that marriage involves many obligations which they find tiresome, and taking another wife merely doubles them. Two houses have to be built—sometimes in different villages—they have to help in cultivating two sets of gardens, and provide clothing for two wives. The introduction of cash and a wider range of consumer goods competing for a man's resources now provides an additional dis-incentive for polygyny. A man does not appear to gain prestige by the possession of many wives. One village headman in Chapananga's area had fifteen wives; this amused the local inhabitants and he was ridiculed rather than respected. In Tombondera out of a total of forty-seven men (nineteen of whom are Christian) thirty-three have one wife, eleven have two and one has three wives. Polygyny is not a major factor in recruitment to simple

---

[18] The Rev. J. V. Taylor tells me that in his experience this is also the case in the majority of African sects in Uganda and the Northern Rhodesia Copperbelt.

116 SECTARIANISM IN SOUTHERN NYASALAND

secessionist sects, though serial monogamy may be—most men have no desire for more than one wife at a time. These African sects do admit those who have been expelled from other churches or sects for taking a second wife, provided they are living with only one of them at the time they are admitted. With this exception their attitude towards marriage is the same as that of the missions.

The Ethiopian Church, on the other hand, does permit polygyny, citing the Israelites in the Old Testament as a precedent. I have heard some of its members recommending this sect to their friends and neighbours for this reason—but unfortunately my contact with its congregations was insufficient to assess the number of polygynous marriages contracted by its members.

Dislike of Christian/Western marriage regulations introduced by White missionaries is not of paramount importance in the development of African sects in Southern Nyasaland. It may be an important source of recruitment to the Ethiopian Church, but in 1958–9 this sect had only ten out of a total of 576 congregations in Mlanje.

The fact that many African sects require no examination before baptizing new members may attract pagans wishing to join a congregation. On the other hand, as the source of recruitment to simple secessionist sects is largely dissident members of other congregations rather than pagans—this is not a major factor in recruiting members. To understand the simple secessionists' attractions we must consider their attraction for people who are already Christian rather than for pagans.

There are two main sources of recruitment to simple secessionist congregations. Firstly, when an elder or deacon starts a congregation of his own by transferring his allegiance to an African sect those members of the original congregation who find him a more attractive leader than its local minister may accompany him. Where congregations split in this way a large proportion appears to join the African sect,[19] though some may return later. Secondly, once a congregation has been formed in this way it may expand through the recruitment of those who have been expelled from White missions. Often, however, congregations in African sects, in fact, contract rather than expand shortly after the initial secession which led to their formation. People may become disillusioned with the new local minister, and

---

[19] It is difficult to assess the actual numbers involved in any one instance. The two congregations are usually hostile to each other and to have gained an entry into an area through one congregation makes it difficult to achieve *rapport* with the other. One is left with a one-sided picture.

THE SECT AS A SOCIAL GROUP 117

may gradually drift back to the original congregation—or they may cease to take part in the activities of either.

The attractions of the Ethiopian Church are rather different. It has nativistic elements in its doctrines and specifically rejects some Christian/Western values. This clearly attracts some followers: members of the Ethiopian Church emphasize that they keep the traditional rules of behaviour over such things as sexual prohibitions and that the young people's failure to keep these rules is responsible for the present troubles in the country. Although the membership of the Ethiopian Church is small compared with the total membership of the simple secessionist sects, it expanded rapidly in the Southern Province after the 'Declaration of a State of Emergency' in 1959. This may have been associated with an increase in tension between Africans and Whites leading more people to reject White values. From my limited experience of the Ethiopian Church, its sources of recruitment appear to differ in three main respects from those of the simple secessionists. Firstly, it attracts pagans rather than those who are already Christians to its congregations; secondly, the average age of the members of its congregations is very much higher; and thirdly, it appeals to men as much as, if not more than, women.

Social control in the sects

The Church of Scotland and the Protestant sects are seen by informants as 'legalistic'—i.e. with a strong emphasis on rules of behaviour and prohibitions. When a religious group which is unfamiliar to informants is mentioned in discussion the first question that they ask is often 'What are its rules?' This emphasis is also reflected in the name by which the Ethiopian Church is often known to outsiders—the *Zoipa Citani* church (the 'Do Bad Things' church), that is, the church which ignores the rules of the missionaries. All the Protestants in Southern Nyasaland prohibit the drinking of alcohol and some have a rule against smoking. The puritan principles of the Victorian Nonconformists were exported to the mission field and have remained there.

If these rules are to be kept there must be sanctions upholding them. Supernatural sanctions commonly support the social order of religious groups. These sanctions are formalized in the Roman Catholic Church, where priests have divine authority to hear confessions and impose penances. In the Protestant organizations the supernatural sanction is diffuse and less formal. Those transgressing the laws of the

118   SECTARIANISM IN SOUTHERN NYASALAND

church or sect are constantly threatened in sermons with dire punishments on the 'Day of Judgement'. As Robert Graves has remarked:
'The threats of hell's quenchless flames and the satyro-morphic view
of Satan are now chiefly used for export purposes to Kenya and the
Congo Basin',[20] and, one might add, to Nyasaland. In one sermon to a
congregation in the Faithful Church of Christ, Severe stressed the
need for obedience to 'the laws of God' and went on to say that this
meant obedience to the elders and ministers of the sect. It is, of course,
difficult to assess the effects of such diffuse sanctions on actual behaviour. One member of the Ethiopian Church, however, referring to
members of the Church of Scotland remarked: '*Sali kuopa Mulungu
iai, ali kuopa anthu basi*'—'They are not afraid of God, they are only
afraid of men.'

Public opinion may be invoked as a sanction. In the Faithful
Church of Christ confessions are occasionally heard in public before
the Eucharist is celebrated. I only heard one such confession. During
a service at Chaima village Abesse, an unmarried girl, came for-
ward and spoke to the minister, who then related what he had heard
to the congregation. Abesse had been to a (Western-type) dance where
two men had fought because she danced with one and not the other.
She stated that she had come to confess that the fight was her fault,
that if she had not been at the dance, then it would not have occurred.
The minister then asked those members of the congregation willing
to forgive her to raise a hand; practically the entire congregation did
so. The minister then told her not to go to a dance again. In this
particular case it is difficult to imagine that it was not without a certain
amount of pride that Abesse related how two men had fought for her
favours. Other sects do not appear to have this institution. In conversation with Severe afterwards he told me that it was only a sin
committed in public which required a public confession. He suggested
that if he became drunk at a beer-drink and members of his sect
learnt about it he would have to make a public confession—if they
did not then no such confession was necessary!

Those transgressing the rules of both White and African sects may
be brought before an 'ecclesiastical' court composed of members of
the congregation.[21] Here a minister or the head of the sect acts in a

---

[20] Graves, 1927, p. 12.

[21] Similar courts are found in other parts of Africa—it seems that the sects in
Southern Nyasaland are not the only ones to have a distinctly legalistic outlook.
(See, for instance, Pauw, op. cit., p. 218.)

THE SECT AS A SOCIAL GROUP

judicial capacity. The minister is advised by the elders and deacons and any member of the congregation who wishes to may express his views on the case. There are, however, few sanctions, short of expulsion from the congregation, which such a court can employ. Their significance seems to lie in the fact that the congregation meets together and the offences become public knowledge. Makuta, a pagan in N. A. Nazombe's area, was married to a member of the Church of Scotland and complained to the local minister about his wife's behaviour, asking that he should hear the case against her in front of the congregation; clearly he felt that this would impose sanctions on her. In the event it did not and they became divorced soon afterwards.

A sanction which may be employed against office-holders is the removal, or threat of removal, from office. Cedrick was a deacon in the Zambesi Mission at Tombondera. This sect has a rule against smoking, and during a year when his gardens produced insufficient food he bought cigarettes in bulk and re-sold them at a profit. He was brought before a court composed of members and officials of the congregation and deprived of his office. Cedrick remained a member of the congregation—the only one in the village.

In the Faithful Church of Christ the threat of removal from office is a powerful sanction wielded by the head of the sect. The sect receives financial support from one of the Churches of Christ in California and a large proportion of the money is used to pay ministers', and in some cases local ministers' stipends. Some ministers in 1958–9 received twenty-five dollars per month, a large amount in relation to the general level of wages in Nyasaland, and one which in view of their low educational standards they would be unlikely to receive elsewhere. Deprivation of office here means deprivation of a not inconsiderable stipend. Severe has effective control over the allocation of the sect's finances.

All the religious groups are voluntary associations and so the sanction of expulsion can easily be applied to erring members. I have already stressed that this sanction is not infrequently employed in the White Protestant missions. On the other hand, the fact that the sects are voluntary associations means that ministers cannot impose personal sanctions on unwilling followers—the followers may easily leave his congregation.

Administration in the sects

The administration of the African sects is modelled upon that of

120   SECTARIANISM IN SOUTHERN NYASALAND

the White missions, and the attempts made to copy the details of procedure used in a Western administrative system sometimes lead to a caricature of that system. Meetings of ministers and other officials take place at regular intervals and letters are constantly passing to and fro between the various congregations. The following account of a meeting held at the headquarters of the Faithful Church of Christ illustrates the importance which is attached to the correct procedure.

The meeting was described by Severe, the head of the sect, as an 'Extra-Ordinary Meeting' (the ordinary meetings being held quarterly). It was held in a schoolroom at the headquarters of the sect at Wendewende, starting at 10.30 a.m. on a Saturday. Severe sat at a table facing the remainder of the ministers, who were sitting on benches. The meeting started with a hymn, which was followed by the Lord's Prayer and then Severe read Romans xvi. 16 ('Salute one another with a kiss. The Churches of Christ salute you.')—an oft-quoted passage in the Faithful Church of Christ, though the injunction is not carried out.

Severe opened the meeting with an apology for the lack of a typed agenda, saying that the secretary of the sect had gone to his own village for the week-end. He then passed round a piece of paper, asking the officials to sign their names on it as a record of their attendance at the meeting (eleven of them were present). While this was circulating he introduced the first item of business as 'The Presidential Address' [sic], using the English term, although the meeting was conducted in Nyanja. This introduced the subject of a minister's disobedience. Lupya, who was not present at the meeting, was a minister in charge of a number of congregations in the Cholo District. The local minister of one of those congregations, Chidothe, had been expelled from the Faithful Church of Christ by a previous meeting of ministers for contracting a polygynous marriage. Chidothe, however, continued to hold services in the prayer house, and in this he was supported by a large proportion of his congregation and by Lupya. During the week before the meeting a delegation of ministers had visited him to find out why he was allowing Chidothe to continue to use the prayer house belonging to the Faithful Church of Christ. These ministers were called upon to report on their visit. They stated that Lupya's argument was that he was ignoring the instructions of Severe and the other ministers because, although he was one of the first ministers to be appointed in the Faithful Church of Christ, unlike most other ministers he still did not receive financial support from the United

THE SECT AS A SOCIAL GROUP

States. Other ministers present at the meeting then suggested that Lupya should have brought this complaint to the 'Faculty of Ministers' [sic], and that what he was, in fact, trying to do was to leave the Faithful Church of Christ and to start a sect of his own. After further discussion Severe suggested that another letter be sent to Lypya telling him that four ministers were coming to visit him the following week, and that if he did not enforce Chidothe's expulsion, then he himself would be expelled. This was then put as a motion to the meeting, and, voted upon by a show of hands, it was passed unanimously.

Severe then introduced another subject for discussion. He pointed out that the original prayer house at the headquarters of the sect had been pulled down because it was unsafe, and that they were using the school as a prayer house. Again a formal motion was put that the prayer house should be rebuilt, and was passed unanimously by a show of hands. The building of more schools was then discussed. Severe told the meeting that many village headmen and others had approached him to start a school in their village. He pointed out that the main problem was money, and one of the ministers suggested that each congregation should be asked to contribute a little, and then the Government should be approached for a grant. This was agreed to informally.

The last item to be discussed was the posting of preachers to visit various congregations, and after this had been arranged for the following few weeks, Severe closed the meeting with an extempore prayer.

The whole meeting was characterized by its formality—the 'Presidential Address', the apology for the lack of typed minutes, the circulation of a piece of paper for recording the attendance, the voting procedure, and speakers standing to address the meeting (not a usual procedure at village headmen's courts, and not always done at the Native Authority courts). This may have been partly the result of my attendance at the meeting, but it does appear that those attending were familiar with the procedure, and so it is unlikely that it had been 'laid on' for my special benefit. Even if this had been the case, the point is still clear—the attempt was being made to conduct the meeting as far as possible in accordance with what was considered to be the way in which such a meeting would be conducted by Whites.

Sect economics

Money is required for a variety of purposes by all but the very

122 SECTARIANISM IN SOUTHERN NYASALAND

smallest sects. The White missions and a few of the African sects pay stipends to their ministers and pastors, and also sometimes buy them bicycles to enable them to attend meetings and visit congregations. Ministers who spend much of their time in activities connected with their office may have little opportunity for cultivation of gardens and consequently be partly, at least, dependent upon a stipend for food.

Money is also needed to build prayer houses, schools (although government subsidies may meet some of the cost), and occasionally for ministers' houses. Many prayer houses, however, and almost all those belonging to African sects, are made from wattle and daub and have a thatched roof and mud floor; the only furniture is a table and a few chairs brought in from the local minister's house for each service. Such buildings cost little; they are built by members of the congregation and probably the only items which have to be bought are the larger timbers for the frame of the building. Some prayer houses are more elaborate, being built from Kimberley brick and roofed with corrugated iron. These are more expensive; members of the congregation may make the bricks, but the corrugated iron has to be purchased. A few even more elaborate church buildings with glass windows and permanent furniture have been built in Southern Nyasaland. These are at the headquarters and larger mission stations of the White missions. The only African sect to possess a very elaborate church building is the Providence Industrial Mission at Chiradzulu.

Nyasaland is a poor country. The vast majority of the population of the Southern Province are subsistence cultivators, growing maize, millet, cassava, and rice. Domesticated animals are of minor importance and have not provided a means of amassing wealth. There are two important cash crops, tobacco in the Shire Highlands and cotton in the Shire Valley. Most people grow one of these, but the amount per grower is small. Both cotton and tobacco are sold to the Agricultural Production and Marketing Board, a Government-sponsored organization which also supplies the seed, and most growers received an income of £5–£10 per year. A few 'master farmers' grow more and receive a much larger income, but rarely does this exceed £50 per year. Small amounts of the crops grown for subsistence may also be sold. Cash-cropping has not led to the development of a wealthy class in Southern Nyasaland. The range of economic differentiation among those dependent upon cultivation for their livelihood is limited.

Apart from cash-cropping, small amounts of money may be obtained from fishing on Lake Shirwa. At the time I visited the lake

THE SECT AS A SOCIAL GROUP 123

in 1959 one fisherman had accumulated sufficient capital to buy a small motor-boat, but all the remainder relied upon rather crudely constructed dug-out canoes. Fish trading is an occasional source of money for many men in Mlanje wanting a small amount of cash for a specific purpose. They buy a basket of fish at the lake-shore and transport it, usually by bicycle, to Blantyre and other markets, where they sell the fish singly. Women also may make small amounts of money by brewing beer, either for a beer-drink or to sell to passers-by at the roadside. In both Mlanje and Chapananga's area there are a large number of 'Kantini'. These are small stores of wattle and daub construction, selling cigarettes, candles, paraffin, bicycle spares, cloth, patent medicines, etc. Many of them have been started by labour migrants returning from Rhodesia with a small amount of capital. Few of them, however, provide their owners, who are also subsistence cultivators, with a livelihood. The owners of the larger stores who do make sufficient profit to maintain themselves and their dependants are usually of Asian or Afro-Asian descent.

Wage labour is perhaps the most fruitful source of income in Southern Nyasaland, but the opportunities for employment are limited by the lack of resources for industrial development.[22] In Mlanje the White-owned tea estates provide some opportunities for employment, but there are no estates in Chapananga's area. A steady income can be obtained by working as a Government employee—those with a sufficient standard of education as clerks, agricultural demonstrators, medical aides, etc.—others as labourers. Clerks in 1958–9 earned around £8 per month and labourers around £2. The latter, and indeed some of the former, usually rely on their gardens for at least part of their food supply. Wage labour does not provide opportunities for amassing wealth, though it does enable people to buy some of the consumer goods introduced by the Whites.

The pockets of the members of their congregations are thus not a large source of wealth to the churches and sects operating in Southern Nyasaland. Several White missions have a fixed system of 'dues' which their members are expected to contribute. Failure to do so may eventually lead to expulsion. Those African sects which are entirely

---

[22] There is a considerable amount of labour migration from Nyasaland to the Rhodesias and to a lesser extent to South Africa. According to the 1945 Population census some 3 per cent of the total population of Mlanje and Chikwawa were absent at the time it was taken. In a small sample in Chapananga's area I found that 64 per cent of all the men had been out of the country at some time as labour migrants.

124 SECTARIANISM IN SOUTHERN NYASALAND

dependent upon the financial contributions of their members are generally very poor. The *Kagulu ka Nkhosa*, for instance, has only one wattle and daub prayer house and this has a poorly thatched roof. The head of the sect, the Rev. Rogers, is entirely dependent upon subsistence cultivation for his livelihood, receiving no stipend from members of his congregation. Members of African sects rarely have educational qualifications enabling them to secure regular jobs with a relatively high salary. Such qualifications are obtained at mission schools and those gaining them are rarely subsequently attracted to an African sect.

The White missions receive financial support from their parent bodies in Europe, America, and Australia. In some American missions this support seems to be on a fairly lavish scale. Some African sects also receive money from the United States. Generally, however, the African sects are handicapped by their lack of money. The expansion of the Faithful Church of Christ, which has been much more rapid than the expansion of any other African sect, is due in no small measure to its receipt of American money.

When Joseph Booth established the three 'Industrial Missions' at the end of the last century it was his intention that they should be self-propagating and self-supporting. These intentions have never fully been realized and the Industrial Missions still receive aid from outside the Protectorate. These missions still, however, have plantations from which they derive part of their income. None of the African sects which have seceded from these Industrial Missions have attempted to develop similar plantations. There appear to be three possible explanations for their failure to do so. Firstly, when the Industrial Missions were first established there was less pressure on land than is the case at the present time. Since the increase in population sect leaders would have difficulty in obtaining land for such a project. Secondly, the founders of the seceding sects have seceded from outlying congregations rather than from the headquarters where the plantations are located, and so have little knowledge of their organization. Thirdly, the founders of these sects lacked the capital and the technical knowledge to attempt such a project.

In some parts of Africa, African sects and their leaders have become very wealthy as a result of their commercial activities.[23] This has not

---

[23] See, for instance, the accounts of Bishop Limba and the *Ibandla lika Krestu* in South Africa by Mqotsi and Mkele (1946), and of Aiyetoro in Nigeria, *Nigeria Magazine* (1957).

THE SECT AS A SOCIAL GROUP
125

happened in the African sects in Southern Nyasaland. Severe, the founder of the Faithful Church of Christ, has become one of the more wealthy inhabitants of Mlanje District, but he has not acquired anything like the wealth of African sect leaders in some other parts of the continent. He has been able, by using money sent from the United States, to buy a diesel-operated maize mill, which is worked by a paid employee and is in constant use grinding maize (for payment) for local villagers. His gardens are fairly extensive compared with the average holding in the area (informants suggested that he had been '*wanzeru*' —shrewd—in his acquisition of land) and he is able to employ paid labour to cultivate them. He has not, however, re-invested any of the profit which he has made from these enterprises—but is known locally for his conspicuous consumption. This was the basis of constant complaints by members of the Faithful Church of Christ, who felt that the money should be used to expand the activities of the sect.

There appears to be little economic inducement to become an official or member of an African sect not receiving financial support from outside the Protectorate. Some officials have been expelled from White missions for enriching themselves from mission funds, but the amounts involved have been very small. Pastors or ministers in African sects which receive no financial help may be given occasional gifts by members of their congregation, but the amounts are insignificant.

The sects' relations with outsiders

As religious affiliation does not provide the basis for residential grouping, members of congregations do not live in isolation from other inhabitants of the area. The inhabitants of a single village in Mlanje typically belong to several different congregations, and in Chapananga's area Christians and pagans are to be found living in adjacent households. Christians are members of other social groups in addition to the local congregation, but at the same time congregations often form corporate groups for secular purposes. Christians who are sick, for instance, may appeal to the pastor for help in cultivating their gardens and the task is carried out by members of the congregation working as a group. When a Christian builds a house he first erects the wattle framework and may then ask for the help of the congregation in plastering it; men of the congregation then dig a large hole into which women pour water brought from a nearby river or

126 SECTARIANISM IN SOUTHERN NYASALAND

well. Children then carry the mud which is formed to the house, where other men plaster it on the wattle. No payments are made, but the owner of the house is expected to provide the helpers with fruit or other refreshment to eat while the work is in progress. The local congregation provides the basis for such co-operation, but others who are not members of the congregation may also help. When one house in Tombondera was being plastered in this way a number of pagans were also working—because, they said, of *cibwenzi* (informal friendship). Such co-operative activities take place in the congregations of both White missions and African sects, but there is no equivalent group for pagans, who, if they want help, must rely on ties of personal friendship. Generally the smaller size of the African sect congregations leads to a greater sense of social solidarity and there is a greater amount of co-operation between them in secular contexts than is the case in some of the larger congregations belonging to the White missions.

The funerals of Christians are conducted according to the rites of the particular congregation to which they belong and officials of the congregation take the place of the traditional burial partners. Pagans are, however, allowed to attend Christian funerals, and I heard of no cases of pagans objecting to Christian burial rites being performed for their Christian dependants. I have already pointed out earlier in this chapter how the congregation is now an important group in the regulation of the marriages of its members. The traditional marriage witnesses are, however, still essential regardless of whether they were members of the congregation or not; they have not, like the burial partners, been replaced by officials of the congregation.

Churches and sects, in Southern Nyasaland at least, are not exclusive groups; they aim to have a universal appeal. They are constantly attempting to increase their following by recruiting pagans, and in some cases members of other congregations. Pagans are known as, and indeed refer to themselves as, *akunja* (literally—'those outside'), but they are admitted to almost all a congregation's activities.[24] Those intending to become members of a congregation regularly attend its services, but pagans with no intention of becoming members may also occasionally attend. When a White missionary visited the Zambesi Mission congregation at Tombondera to baptize new members a

---

[24] They are not generally allowed to attend meetings of a congregation when the behaviour of one of its members is being discussed or to receive the sacraments at the Eucharist.

THE SECT AS A SOCIAL GROUP

number of pagans donned their best clothes and attended the service. One old man, a confirmed pagan, who was loud in his ridicule of the Christians for refusing to drink beer, borrowed a complete suit and a bright red cap from his son, who had recently returned from Southern Rhodesia, to attend both the ritual at the riverside and the subsequent service in the prayer house. When a White missionary visits a congregation the village headman, whether he is a member or not, is often invited to attend the service, and if he does so is given a seat with the elders at the front of the prayer house.

There is little apparent hostility between pagans and Christians, and as well as sometimes attending their services pagans also observe Christian festivals, albeit rather differently from the Christians. Both cease work on Sundays (except for the Seventh-day sects, who regard Saturday as the Sabbath) even in areas well away from White employers. It is the day for services in the prayer houses and beer-drinks elsewhere. The phrase 'to make Christmas' is widely used by both Christians and pagans to denote any festive social activity. Chirapula, the pagan *mwini dziko* of N. A. Nazombe's area, when describing how offerings are made to the spirits of his matrilineage, remarked, *'tili kupanga Christmas* ('We make Christmas'). Many pagans know something of Christian doctrines and many are only too willing to send their children to Christian schools; often the handicap is finding the school fees. This lack of hostility between Christians and pagans is possibly associated with the lack of any strong tribal traditions in the area. Pagan rites have generally not come in for the same strong opposition on the part of missionaries as the Kikuyu girls' initiation ceremonial, for instance. Pagans do not feel themselves to belong to a group in opposition to the Christians.

There is little hostility between the White Protestant missions; most are now members of the Nyasaland Federation of Missions, and the accusations of proselytization, which sometimes occur between Catholics and Protestants and which the Church of Scotland levelled at Joseph Booth when he first established the Zambesi Industrial Mission, are now rare between Protestant missions.

There is little interaction between White missions and African sects at the official level and generally there is little hostility between them. Part of this is due to the fact that Protestant missionaries are frequently unaware of the existence of African sects—they are not spectacular with colourful uniforms or exotic rituals—and their attempts to be as far as possible like the White sects make them

128 SECTARIANISM IN SOUTHERN NYASALAND

relatively inconspicuous amongst the large number of prayer houses in Mlanje. Catholic missionaries are generally more aware of the existence of the African sects, but do not regard them as a serious threat; several of those whom I met suggested, as we have seen quite rightly, that they had seceded from the Protestant missions to become 'chiefs' of their own churches.

The leaders of many African sects are friendly towards each other —there is no manifestation of hostility between them, though equally there is no form of co-operation between them. The exceptions to this are relations between the sects which have split to form new ones. Hostility, for instance, exists between the Faithful Church of Christ and the African Church of Christ from which Severe seceded. The same is true at the level of the local congregation; relations between members of different congregations are not generally hostile except where one has been formed by secession from the other. This is the case, for instance, in Chaima village, where the Faithful Church of Christ congregation was formed by secession from the Sons of God. Chimenya, the minister in charge of the Faithful Church of Christ congregation, avoided all social contact with the local minister of the Sons of God, as did most members of his congregation. Where such conflicts exist they seem to remain restricted to the level at which they took place, Severe, for instance, still maintains friendly relations with the head of the Sons of God sect.

IX

NYASALAND SECTARIANISM IN PERSPECTIVE—SOME COMPARISONS

IN the Introduction it was stated that sectarianism, widespread in Christendom, had characterized the history of Christianity. It is widespread in modern Africa, but far from universal. Thus it is found in some parts of Southern Nyasaland and not in others, in Mlanje, for instance, but not in Chapananga's area, in the rural areas of the Shire Highlands, but not in the Blantyre/Limbe urban area. In Nyasaland the presence or absence of African sects appears to be partly associated with a number of socio-economic factors. Furthermore the type of sect which is formed in Southern Nyasaland is also associated with the socio-economic background of the area and the type of missions which have established themselves within it.

Disagreements or conflicts between members of a religious group do not necessarily lead to secession and the formation of a new one. It has already been noted that two prophecies of a Messianic nature were recorded in Southern Nyasaland, but no new religious group was formed with these prophecies as its charter. Similarly Pauw records the existence of a prophetess Botlhale, an Anglican, in the Taung Reserve. In 1909 she was possessed by the 'Spirit of God' and was able to prescribe treatment for the sick and to make magical use of consecrated water. She was especially remembered as a prophetess with abilities as a rainmaker. Botlhale never organized a church or a congregation of her own, but when she died in 1952 she was buried by the African United Church.[1]

In Uganda a revival movement started within the Anglican Church about 1929, which spread through much of Uganda and later into Kenya. It was a protest against hypocrisy in the Anglican Church and introduced public confessions. This movement did not lead to the development of a new sect in Uganda, but in Kenya it was the basis of establishing the Church of Christ in Africa.[2] This is possibly associated with the different types of power structures found in Uganda and Kenya; it may also be associated with the different types of power structures of the various missions working in the two countries.[3]

---

[1] Pauw, 1960, pp. 48–49. [2] Welbourn, 1961, pp. 9–10. [3] See below, pp. 140–2.

130   SECTARIANISM IN SOUTHERN NYASALAND

In Southern Nyasaland, as we have seen, sectarianism is found in Mlanje, but not in Chapananga's area, and there are considerable differences in the amount of contact each area has had with missionaries, this being partly the result of climatic factors. Only two White missions operate in Chapananga's area: the diversity of White sects which provides an example for sectarianism in Mlanje is absent here. The population density is much higher in Mlanje than in Chapananga's area, settlements are dispersed and communications easier. A new sect in Mlanje has a more populous catchment area from which to recruit followers. Taylor and Lehmann have pointed out the contrast between sparsely populated Northern Rhodesia and densely populated Nyasaland in the devolution of authority within missions. They suggest that in Nyasaland missionaries have been able to establish many congregations, placing Africans in sole charge but without having to leave them unsupervised for months at a time. In Northern Rhodesia the sparse population has encouraged the establishment of large mission stations with boarding schools, while the remainder of the work is carried out by itinerant unordained workers.[4] The greater devolution of authority in Nyasaland, and particularly in Mlanje, is a factor in the development of sectarianism: the African ecclesiastical official becomes a person of status and consequently there is competition for these offices.

In Chapter VIII I attempted to show how African sects provide opportunities for positions of power and prestige for those unable to achieve such positions in the present political hierarchy. I also sought to indicate that the lower density of population in Chapananga's area has important repercussions on the political structure, that achievement of status is still possible here, and suggested that this is associated with the lack of sectarianism.

Sectarianism in Nyasaland is characteristic of the rural area of the Shire Highlands, but not of the urban area. The situation here is the reverse of that found among the Tswana by Pauw. The headquarters of the African sects found in the Taung Reserve are mainly located on the Witwatersrand, while the older missions in South Africa mostly originated in the rural areas and spread into the towns.[5] In Southern Nyasaland many of the missions started work in what is now the urban area of Blantyre/Limbe and then spread into the rural areas, while the African sects started in the rural areas and have remained

---

[4] Taylor and Lehmann, 1961, pp. 20-21.   [5] Pauw, op. cit. p. 105.

NYASALAND SECTARIANISM IN PERSPECTIVE 131

there. I suggested in Chapter III that the type of urban development in Nyasaland was very different from the Witwatersrand; it is commercial rather than industrial and the White missions preceded rather than followed the development of the town. In Nyasaland a sect official must have a church building if he is to be truly regarded as an official. The cost of erecting such buildings in the urban area is prohibitive for the African sects, thus the 'homeless' African congregations found in the industrial Copperbelt and the Witwatersrand are not found in Blantyre/Limbe. Moreover, in Blantyre/Limbe (though I have not myself carried out fieldwork there), there are apparently many more ways of gaining prestige. The traditional values have persisted less in the town and the possession of a following is less a mark of status than in the rural areas. Here prestige can more easily be achieved through wealth, occupation, prowess in sport or music, etc.

In the larger urban areas of Central Africa many White missions also have substantial White congregations. In these circumstances missionaries may find themselves placed in the difficult position of having to serve both a White and an African congregation. Often their primary allegiance is to their White congregations, by whom their salaries are paid, and difficulties sometimes arise over the admission of Africans to services for Whites.[6] This leads to accusations of hypocrisy and ultimately to the development of African sects supported by some of the more educated members of the African community. The White population of Blantyre/Limbe is not large enough for the White churches and sects to become anything other than fundamentally missionary in outlook. There is one exception to this; the Anglican Church has a church building and priests who cater primarily for the White population. This, however, is not a source of conflict, since there are very few African Anglicans in the area.[7] Relations between White and African members of churches do not appear to have been a factor in sectarianism in Southern Nyasaland.[8]

In the last chapter I attempted to show some patterns in the incidence of sect membership among various categories of the population. I pointed out that both White missions and African sects, with the

---

[6] Taylor and Lehmann, op. cit., Chapter 8.

[7] Bettison did not record any in his peri-urban survey. (See Bettison, 1958, pp. 54–57.)

[8] Conflicts have arisen in the Church of Scotland over the relations between the White officials and their White and African members. These, however, have resulted in dissatisfaction among the White members rather than among the Africans.

132   SECTARIANISM IN SOUTHERN NYASALAND

exception of the Ethiopian Church, had a higher membership of women than of men. This numerical predominance of women members is also found in churches and sects in other parts of Africa. In Tanganyika, for instance, 'women outnumbered the men by more than three to one in the congregations in Ngonde (where many men were away as labour migrants) and by three to two in the Moravian congregations in Nyakyusa'.[9] Among the Swazi, too, there are more women who are Christians than men, and Kuper records: 'I came across no instance, nor could any be recalled, where the father (of a school child) was a Christian and the mother a pagan.[10] On the Taung Reserve 74 per cent of members of eleven 'churches connected with Europeans' were women and in none of them were men numerically predominant. Sixty-two per cent of the nineteen 'Separatist Churches' were women, but in three of them men, in fact, outnumbered women.[11] The sects in Southern Nyasaland thus conform in this respect to the general pattern reported from other parts of East and Southern Africa.

In Europe and the United States a correlation between religious affiliation and social class has been noted, the lower social classes (based upon the prestige ratings of occupational categories) having a higher incidence of sect membership.[12]

There is some evidence of similar trends developing in parts of Africa. It has been suggested that in Freetown, Sierra Leone, people move up the scale from the smaller sects to the Anglican Church as they move up the socio-economic class system.[13] In South Africa 'some class distinctions begin to appear in the Independent Churches on the Rand. The upper class—the Bantu intelligentsia—editors, doctors, and lawyers—will be found in the African Methodist Episcopal Church, whereas at the other end of the scale Zionist sects take care of the uneducated.'[14] In both these cases the smaller sects perform rituals in which 'emotionalism' or possession plays a large part. This is not the case among the simple secessionist sects in Southern Nyasaland, but here also some correlation can be discerned between socio-economic class and religious affiliation. The process of socio-economic class differentiation has, however, not proceeded very far in Southern Nyasaland, which lacks the natural resources for the acquisition of wealth. The socio-economic distinctions that do exist are very much

---

[9] Wilson, 1959, p. 168.　　[10] Kuper, 1946, p. 183.
[11] Pauw, op. cit., pp. 96, 97.　　[12] See, for instance, Dynes, 1955.
[13] Porter, 1953, p. 12.　　[14] Sundkler, 1961, p. 86.

NYASALAND SECTARIANISM IN PERSPECTIVE 133

a matter of educational difference. The *élite* of Southern Nyasaland are the clerks, the teachers, and the dispensers, etc., and having received their education in mission schools the members of this *élite* are not generally attracted to the African sects. The leader of the Providence Industrial Mission, Dr. Daniel Malekebu, is highly educated, and Severe, the founder of the Faithful Church of Christ, has a Standard Eight certificate of education, but apart from these the officials and members of the African sects are almost entirely drawn from the rank and file of subsistence cultivators. The headmaster of the African Nyasa Church School, who is sufficiently qualified to receive a Government subsidy, is a Seventh-day Adventist. Phombeya, the founder of this sect, told me that he would have preferred to have appointed a member of his own sect, but none was sufficiently qualified. Similarly the secretary/typist at the headquarters of the Faithful Church of Christ was a member of the Church of Scotland who stated that he had no intention of changing his allegiance. He told me that he had only come to Wendewende because there was a shortage of jobs for clerks in the area.

As I have indicated in Chapter III, a few informants suggested that there was a correlation between tribal and religious affiliation. They suggested that the majority of the members of African sects were Nguru, while the Nyanja supported only the Roman Catholic Church and the Church of Scotland. I have already shown that I found no evidence to support this contention; apart from the fact that the majority of Moslems are Yao, there does not appear to be any relation between tribal and religious affiliation.

Southern Nyasaland differs in this respect from some other parts of Africa where such correlations do, or did, exist. Schapera, writing of the Tswana, states: 'Missionaries . . . by about 1870 were established in all the larger tribes. They usually succeeded fairly soon in converting the chief. . . . Until fairly recently many tribes had misssionaries of one denomination only, so that the Christianity of, say, the Ngwaketse (Congregationalist) differed in some features from that of the Kgatla (Dutch Reformed) or the Malete (Lutheran). Now . . . denominational monopolies have largely disappeared . . .'[15] In Buganda 'although chieftainships were rigidly divided between the Roman, Anglican, and small Moslem parties, the dominant place in native administration and education has been held by the

---

[15] Schapera, 1953, p. 58.

134 SECTARIANISM IN SOUTHERN NYASALAND

Anglicans.'[16] Sundkler has described the close links existing between some of the Zionist sects in Swaziland and the Swazi paramount chief.[17] In all these cases the tribe is a single state (the Tswana tribes are defined in this way), and the predominance of one denomination has resulted from the conversion of the head of the state to that denomination. When missionaries first arrived in Southern Nyasaland there were no state structures through which they could make their influence felt. The political organization of the area consisted of a number of petty unstable chieftaincies; to convert the head of one of these had little influence on the chieftaincy as a whole. When the Church of Scotland mission was first established in Blantyre it provided a sanctuary for aboriginal Nyanja from the ravages of the slave-raiding Yao, but subsequent population movements have obliterated any correlation between tribe and religious affiliation which might have resulted from this. Likewise the African sects in Mlanje have not attempted to any extent to work through political officials. When Chilembwe was planning the 1915 rising he attempted to gain the support of some Mlanje chiefs, but met with scant success.[18] Today none of the chiefs in Mlanje are members of African sects.

Welbourn has traced the relationship between two of the most important African sects in Buganda and the state organization. Here Church and State have been closely connected. The Bamalaki, a sect which seceded from the Anglican Church, was founded by Mugema, who 'was by inheritance, one of the largest landholders in the country, as head of the monkey clan standing in close ritual relationship to the Kabaka and as a county chief the one remaining personal link, below the Kabaka, between the ancient clan system and the more modern system of centralized administration. Reuben Spartas (who established the African Greek Orthodox Church in Uganda), though the son only of a village headman, is one of the best educated and most able men of his generation. Both are deeply involved in the political and social issues of their day.'[19] Both Mugema's and Spartas's secessions from the Anglican Church were bound up with their relationship with the Ganda State, with which it was closely associated. As the administrative hierarchy in Southern Nyasaland has not been associated with any particular religious group, there is no parallel to this situation. Here both Church and State provide positions of status,

---

[16] Welbourn, op. cit., p. 16.
[18] Shepperson and Price, 1958, p. 251.
[17] Sundkler, op. cit., pp. 316–19.
[19] Welbourn, op. cit., p. 15.

NYASALAND SECTARIANISM IN PERSPECTIVE 135

but conflicts in one do not have direct repercussions in the other.

In some parts of Africa there has been a close association between African sects and nationalist political associations. This seems particularly true of Kenya, where Leakey has described the connexions between the Kikuyu Independent Churches and the Kenya Central Association in the early history of Mau-Mau.[20] On the other hand, such links are far from universal. Sundkler sums up the position in South Africa by saying: 'Claims that "political" reasons are behind the Separatist Church movement miss the mark. The few instances of radical party affiliations of certain Ethiopian or Zionist groups do not offer sufficient proof of any definite political trends; and even admitting the existence of much outspoken anti-White propaganda in most Independent Churches, one should not forget that the attitude of the leaders and masses of these Ethiopians and Zionists has on the whole been loyal, not least during the trying experiences of war. A different question altogether is that the Separatist Church movement both in its Ethiopian and Zionist form is often nationalistic. The term "Ethiopian" has definite nationalistic connotations.'[21]

In Southern Nyasaland the founder of the Providence Industrial Mission, John Chilembwe, was the instigator of the 1915 rising, and the history of the rising and the events leading up to it recorded by Shepperson and Price (1958) is closely bound up with the early history of the sect. After its experience in 1915 the Government was very suspicious of the African sects (and indeed of some White ones), regarding them as potential centres of sedition. Today, however, the situation is rather different. Although the Ethiopian Church, and to a lesser extent the two African Seventh-day Baptist sects, express Africanist sentiments, they are not major foci of anti-White or anti-Government activity. Periodically members of the Seventh-day Baptists clash with the administration, particularly over the payment of taxes and the enforcement of agricultural rules, but so do many people who are not members of African sects. Some Seventh-day Baptist ministers and members have been arrested for failing to carry out Government regulations, a failure which they justify with reference to the Bible, but other members of these sects do not blatantly refuse to obey Government ordinances.

The centre of opposition to the Government in 1958–9 was not the

---

[20] Leakey, 1952, p. 91. (See also Welbourn, op. cit., Chapter 8.)
[21] Sundkler, op. cit., p. 295.

136   SECTARIANISM IN SOUTHERN NYASALAND

African sects but the Nyasaland African National Congress. This was a much greater threat to the Government than the activities of Seventh-day Baptists and members of the Ethiopian Church. Religious protests and political protests tended to be found in separate organizations and there was no overt connexion between the two. Active participation in Congress activities was not apparently more widespread among members of African sects than among members of other religious groups. Shepperson and Price suggest that 'African organization in Nyasaland has assumed the form of religious separatism, often with a distinctly political air', and go on to say: 'In general, as the Nyasaland disturbances of 1953 indicated, all forms of political organization in the Protectorate tend to express themselves in Christian forms: Bible quotation, prayer at meetings, and a general pulpiteering structure of activities to secure effective action.'[22] In 1958–9 it was not the African sects who were the dominant force in this activity, but the Church of Scotland.[23] It would, however, I think, be wrong to attach too much significance to the Christian elements which appear in political meetings. These meetings are held on Sundays—but this is the only day on which employees have a complete day's holiday. The meetings are likely to be more religious in tone than contemporary political meetings in the United Kingdom —they are conducted by the educated *élite*, and almost the only source of education in Nyasaland is the Christian missions.

I suggested in Chapter VII that the African National Congress and the African sects may be alternative avenues to office and the acquisition of a following. This may explain the lack of overt connexions between them.[24] Pauw suggests that the lack of violently anti-White sentiments in the African churches on the Taung Reserve is associated with the lack of large-scale wars in the history of the area and the absence of a strong indigenous military organization.[25] On the other hand, the fact that the Zulu did possess a strong indigenous military

[22] Shepperson and Price, op. cit., pp. 412–13.

[23] 'The only one of the present-day missions to which we need specifically refer, since it is the only one which plays any part in the political life of the country, is the Church of Central Africa (Presbyterian)'. (Devlin, 1959, p. 8.) 'It [the issue of Federation with the Rhodesias] has unfortunately contributed very largely to a cleavage between the Government and the Church of Scotland missions.' (Devlin, op. cit., p. 23.)

[24] cf. Taylor and Lehmann's statement that in Nchanga (N. Rhodesia) no Congress leader was an office-bearer in any church in 1958. (Taylor and Lehmann, op. cit., p. 168.)

[25] Pauw, op. cit., p. 234.

NYASALAND SECTARIANISM IN PERSPECTIVE 137

organization, and, as Sundkler has pointed out,[26] that there is generally a lack of seditious activities in the Zulu churches, appears to suggest that this is not the crucial factor. It seems that a more important factor may be the lack of any concerted attempt on the part of missionaries to eradicate any specific pagan rituals which then become a focus of tribal loyalties. A further factor may be the lack of any other institutions through which opposition to Whites can be mobilized. When Chilembwe led the 1915 rising, churches and sects were the only groups which encompassed the population of more than one chieftaincy. If concerted opposition to the Whites was to be aroused the African sect was the only group through which it could be done. Increasing contact with a Western way of life later led to a greater degree of specialization and specifically political associations were formed; these have replaced the African sect as the centre of opposition to the Whites.

In Southern Nyasaland the predominant feature of African sectarianism has been the development of what I have termed simple secessionist sects. I came into contact with one synthetist sect, the only one of this type, so far as I am aware, operating in Mlanje. I did not come into contact with any of the 'healing' type of sects so common in South Africa; it appears that two of the African sects in Mlanje with which I had no contact may fall into this category and that these have, in fact, been introduced into Nyasaland from South Africa.

The distribution of different types of African sects in East, Central and Southern Africa appears to be influenced by three major sets of factors: firstly, the indigenous power structure and religious beliefs and practices, secondly, the type of missions operating in the area and, in particular, their power structure, and, thirdly, the nature and amount of White settlement in the area.

Pauw discusses an 'important difference between Separatism in Taung and among the Zulu, viz. the absence of such a nativistic trend as that found among the Zulu Zionists'. He goes on to say: 'The absence of such distinct nativistic trends in Taung must probably be related to the advanced stage of disintegration of the traditional culture. A traditionally less elaborate ancestor cult among the Tswana may also be responsible for this difference.'[27] It is significant in this context that the one sect in Mlanje exhibiting nativistic features, the Ethiopian Church, was started by an Ngoni in the Central Province.

---

[26] op. cit., p. 295.   [27] Pauw, op. cit., p. 234.

S.S.N.–K

138 SECTARIANISM IN SOUTHERN NYASALAND

The Ngoni had a more elaborate ancestral cult than the Nyanja, Yao or Nguru, and appear to have retained stronger tribal traditions than the tribes in the Southern Province. Moreover, the founder of the Ethiopian Church himself spent some twenty-seven years in the Union of South Africa. The Ethiopian Church did not originate in the social background of Southern Nyasaland. Once established, however, it did attract recruits from this area, and expanded particularly rapidly at the time relations between Whites and Africans became characterized by tension and distrust in 1958–9.

In the Zulu Zionist sects, and, in fact, in some sects in Europe and the United States, baptism by total immersion is frequently associated with divine healing. All the African and White sects in southern Nyasland practise baptism by total immersion, but only the Assemblies of God, of the sects with which I had contact, stresses the importance of healing. This may, I think, be related to indigenous values. In traditional Zulu society there were close links between religion and health, and 'there is an obvious parallel between the Zulu diviner and the Zionist prophet, a parallel to which heathen and Christian Zulu frequently refer'.[28] Similarly in the Lower Congo, where one of the features of the Kimbangist movement was the emphasis on healing, this was carried out by prophets who were possessed by 'the Spirit'. Possession or dissociation was also a feature of the traditional way of life in this area and was taken over into the Kimbangist movement.[29] Spirit possession does not appear to have been important in Southern Nyasaland, and so there is no basis in the traditional value system for the healing prophets now found in some other parts of the continent.

The absence of messianic sects in Southern Nyasaland is striking. The 'black Christ' ideology found in South Africa and in Kimbangism is not found here. There are some parallels between John Chilembwe and Simon Kimbangu, but the latter has become a messiah in a way that Chilembwe has never done. Both were leaders of Protestant sects which became centres of anti-White discontent. As a result Kimbangu was banished from his home area and imprisoned in Elisabethville for many years,[30] while Chilembwe was killed attempting to evade capture after the 1915 rising.[31] After he had been banished from the Lower Congo, Kimbangu became a focus of wor-

---

[28] Sundkler, op. cit., p. 109.   [29] Andersson, 1958, p. 60.
[30] Andersson, op. cit.   [31] Shepperson and Price, op. cit., pp. 316–17.

NYASALAND SECTARIANISM IN PERSPECTIVE 139

ship, the Kimbangist sects placed him alongside Christ, and as God's apostle it was believed that he would return to rule the Congo. 'He is . . . a prophet with Messianic features that increase.'[32] 'All God's promises will be consummated in and through Simon Kimbangu.'[33] After Chilembwe's death a legend arose that he, too, would return to Nyasaland to drive out the Europeans.[34] This, however, was not generally expected to be a miraculous return; it appears that the disposal of Chilembwe's body had been carried out so quietly that many people refused to believe that he was dead. The legend slowly died. John Chilembwe is still well remembered in Nyasaland—'He was our first leader,' one Congress official told me—but although he is remembered it is not as a supernatural figure. The Providence Industrial Mission which he founded still prospers, but the focus of worship is Christ—not John Chilembwe; its doctrine remains essentially within the main stream of Protestant Christianity. Chilembwe is a hero, but no more—he is not a messiah.

In South Africa, too, sect leaders have become 'messiahs' of their followers. The most famous of these is probably Isaiah Shembe, who, after his death and 'resurrection' in 1935, was regarded by his African Nazarite followers as the Saviour of the Africans in the way that Christ is the Saviour of the Whites.

The failure of the legend which surrounded Chilembwe to develop into a messianic myth seems to be connected with the fact that Chilembwe was not a prophet. He did not start the Providence Industrial Mission as the result of a supernatural revelation to him that he should do so. His position as head of the sect did not depend on charismatic qualities with which his followers believed him to have been endowed by God; he had no abilities as a healer. His position in the P.I.M. depended very much upon the fact that he had been to the United States and was thus familiar with the ways of the Whites. Kimbangu and Shembe, on the other hand, both left mission churches as a result of divine revelations to them; they were, in fact, prophets, believed from the beginning to have been endowed by God with charisma. In the indigenous system of values in Southern Nyasaland, supernatural revelation does not appear to have been a basis of power —consequently neither has it been a basis of power in African sects in this area. The type of sect from which the 'Black Christ ideology'

---

[32] Andersson, op. cit., p. 193.   [33] loc. cit., p. 194.
[34] Shepperson and Price, loc. cit.

140 SECTARIANISM IN SOUTHERN NYASALAND

develops has thus not been a feature of sectarianism in Southern Nyasaland.

I have suggested in previous chapters that the preponderance of the simple secessionist type among the African sects in Southern Nyasaland is associated with three factors: (1) A struggle for positions of leadership and authority and the withdrawal of opportunities for achieving such positions in the political system. (2) The lack of strong tribal sentiments in the area and the desire amongst a large proportion of the population to adopt as far as possible a way of life which they consider to be Western. (3) The diffuse nature of the distribution of power in the White sects in the area.

Although the Roman Catholic Church is the largest single religious group in Southern Nyasaland, no secessionist sects have developed from it, and, furthermore, the amount of recruitment to these sects from this source is relatively very small. I have suggested that this is associated with their hierarchical power structure based upon the doctrine of Apostolic Succession. This lack of secessions from the Roman Catholic Church appears characteristic of Africa generally and not merely of Southern Nyasaland. There are a few exceptions, but they are small in number. One such exception is the *Bana ba Mutima* (the Children of the Sacred Heart), an African sect on the Northern Rhodesian Copperbelt whose activities are described by Taylor and Lehmann.[35] Unfortunately, although it is clear that many aspects of Catholic doctrine are to be found in this sect, no description is given of the way in which their officials are appointed—or of the type of authority which they possess. It is not possible to tell, from the information published, whether or not they have attempted to perpetuate the doctrine of Apostolic Succession.

A comparison between the African Greek Orthodox Church in Uganda, described by Welbourn,[36] which has attempted to perpetuate this doctrine, and the simple secessionist sects of Southern Nyasaland focuses attention on some of the latter's essential features. The contrasts between them are related to the indigenous social structure of the area and with the values behind the distribution of power in the type of missions which have been working in it.

The African Greek Orthodox Church was introduced into Buganda as the result of the activities of Reuben Spartas. Spartas was baptized, as a child, in the Anglican Church and later won a scholarship to

---

[35] Taylor and Lehmann, op. cit., pp. 106–8.   [36] Welbourn, op. cit., Chapter 5.

NYASALAND SECTARIANISM IN PERSPECTIVE 141

King's College, Budo, 'at that time the highest rung of the educational ladder in East Africa'.[37] In 1914 he joined the Army and during the 1920's, by reading the *Negro World*, published by Marcus Garvey, learnt about the African Orthodox Church which had been started among American Negroes in the United States. This church had received its episcopacy from the Eastern Orthodox Church and although the validity of its orders has been questioned by theologians,[38] its members clearly thought them valid. An African Archbishop, Archbishop Alexander, was consecrated and sent to the Union of South Africa. Spartas eventually made contact with him, and in 1929, after he publicly announced that he had broken with the Anglican Church, was appointed a lay-reader for the African Orthodox Church. A protracted series of negotiations followed, resulting in Archbishop Alexander making the journey from South Africa to Uganda in 1931 to train Spartas and a friend and, finally, to ordain them as African Orthodox priests in 1932. The amount of time and money which Spartas spent to ensure that he was properly ordained and given valid orders is in marked contrast with the way in which officials are appointed or have appointed themselves in Nyasaland secessionist sects. Later Spartas learned that the African Orthodox Church was, in fact, a break-away from the Greek Orthodox Church and there followed another series of protracted negotiations for the church under Spartas in Uganda to be recognized by the Orthodox Patriarch of Alexandria. He was eventually successful and the African Orthodox Church in Uganda eventually became a part of the Greek Orthodox Church.

The power structure of Buganda presents a strong contrast to Southern Nyasaland. Politically it consists of a single hierarchical state under the Kabaka. From the religious point of view it is perhaps unique amongst British territories in that missionary activity has been entirely in the hands of the Roman Catholic and Anglican churches, both of which are characterized by a pyramidal power structure. There appears to have been little or no precedent for a man wishing to acquire a following seceding from either church or state. Positions of power were delegated from above; in neither sphere was an office achieved by recruiting followers from below. Spartas disagreed with officials of the Anglican hierarchy, but still wished to operate within what he understood to be the historically valid Church. His studies of

---

[37] Welbourn, op. cit., p. 77.   [38] ibid., pp. 78–79.

142 SECTARIANISM IN SOUTHERN NYASALAND

ecclesiastical history showed him that at an early stage the Christian Church split into East and West and that the Eastern Church, too, had valid authority (i.e. institutionalized charismatic authority). Spartas then spared no effort to acquire this authority.

In Kenya members of the African Independent Pentecostal Association approached the Anglican Bishop of Mombasa in 1933 with a request that he ordain two priests for them. This request was refused. Consequently in 1935 Archbishop Alexander came to Mombasa and ordained African priests, both for the African Orthodox Church and for the African Independent Pentecostal Church.[39] Later deacons were ordained in these sects without a bishop. Welbourn states that 'in the absence of a bishop, Kikuyu independents were prepared—as the A.G.O.C. in Uganda clearly is not—for presbyteral ordination. Like other differences in the two movements this may reflect different patterns of leadership in the tribal societies from which they operate.'[40] In Kenya, as in Southern Nyasaland, there was no pyramidal state structure. On the other hand, a further factor may be involved. Welbourn also states later that 'Law has remarked upon the co-incidence which sent the episcopal Anglican missionaries to Buganda, with its centralized administrative system, and Presbyterians to Kikuyu, where administrative control was far more localized'.[41] Here, as in Southern Nyasaland, the African sects had the example of the European sects with bureaucratic authority to follow.

The African sects in Kenya have tended to multiply, those in Uganda have not. The African Greek Orthodox Church in Uganda has apparently remained one and undivided, while in Kenya it has split into a number of smaller local sects. The 'Revival' in Uganda has been contained within the Anglican Church; in the Nyanza Province of Kenya it has led to the formation of a new sect, the Church of Christ in Africa.

It appears to be only with reluctance that new sects are formed in Uganda; the traditional values associated with the delegation of power from above have persisted. When Mabel Ensor, the White founder of the Mengo Gospel Church, which seceded from the Anglicans, finally left Uganda the sect disintegrated and many of its members returned to the Anglican fold.[42] There does not appear to have been any concerted attempt on the part of African officials to take it over. Southern

---

[39] Welbourn, op. cit., pp. 147–9. [40] ibid., p. 154.
[41] ibid., p. 190. [42] ibid., p. 75.

NYASALAND SECTARIANISM IN PERSPECTIVE   143

Nyasaland presents a vivid contrast to this situation. Here conflicts in the indigenous kinship and residential system, political system, and in the sects lead easily to secession.

Some of the factors leading to simple secession in the sects of Southern Nyasaland also appear to operate on the Taung Reserve. Pauw, writing of this area, states that 'tribal unity was not inviolable and the splitting of tribes is not an uncommon feature in the history of the Tswana'.[43] The Tswana tribe is defined politically and corresponds to the chieftaincy in Southern Nyasaland; both represent in Schapera's terms 'the political community'.[44] The political units of both the Taung Reserve and Southern Nyasaland were thus traditionally both liable to fission and the values supporting such action have persisted. Pauw goes on to say: 'I suggest that under these circumstances, unless the unity of the Church is very strongly accentuated, malcontents easily secede and that this is an important factor in the progressive fragmentation within sectarianism.'[45] Certainly in Southern Nyasaland the unity of the Church has not been demonstrated by missionaries. The fact that in the single administrative District of Mlanje no fewer than eleven White missions are operating provides ample precedents for further African secessions.

In conclusion it would have been valuable to have compared Christianity with the other world religion introduced into Southern Nyasaland—Islam. Sectarianism has occurred in Islam in other parts of the world, but not, so far as I am aware, in Nyasaland. Unfortunately I have no information about Islam in Nyasaland and no accounts of it have been published. Islam is not strong in Mlanje, though there are several Moslem congregations, and it is not represented at all in Chapananga's area.

Moslem informants (I met very few) told me that during the early 1950's a split had occurred in Islam in Nyasaland over the question of singing at funerals. The dispute was settled and unity was soon restored, however, by a visiting 'sheikh' from Zanzibar. Since then there have been no further secessions or attempts at secession.

Several contrasts between Christianity and Islam in Nyasaland, which may be associated with the lack of sectarianism in the latter, suggest themselves. Christianity is associated with the Whites, a group of high status; Islam is not. To hold an office in a Christian congregation is to have a position of prestige in the new values of the

---

[43] Pauw, op. cit., p. 237.   [44] Schapera, 1958, p. 8.   [45] Pauw, loc. cit.

area; this may not be the case to the same extent in Islam. Secondly, from the point of view of Nyasaland Moslems, Islam appears to have a pyramidal power structure centring on Zanzibar—and in this respect is more like the Roman Catholic Church than the sects. Thirdly, there is not the precedent for sectarianism in Islam in Nyasaland that exists in Christianity.

These may or may not be the crucial factors, but I do not possess the data to test them or to make further comparisons. Research into Islam in Nyasaland would not only yield valuable information about the Islamic congregations themselves, a subject about which little has been written at present, but would also shed further light on some of the processes of social change taking place in the territory and of the values associated with them.

APPENDIX A

Analysis of the composition of households in part of Wendewende village containing the headquarters of the Faithful Church of Christ

These hamlets form part of Wendewende village in Chief Nkanda's area in the Mlanje District. Both Chief Mkanda and village headman Wendewende are Mangoche Yao. There are, however, no Yao living in the hamlets under consideration; the majority of the inhabitants are Nguru but there are some Nyanja who have entered the village after the Nguru. Wendewende is a large village consisting of some 430 households, and it is divided into seven sections each of which is under a *nyakwawa*. The hamlets analysed here are under the *nyakwawa* Tapara, a patrilateral cross-cousin of Severe, the founder of the Faithful Church of Christ. The hamlet in which Tapara's household is situated is not included in this analysis, but hamlets composed of relatives of the previous Tapara, Severe's father and the first *nyakwawa*, are included. It appears that the previous Tapara moved into the village some time in the 1930's, bringing with him relatives of his wife as well as his own matrilineal relatives. He moved from a site in the Blantyre District some twenty miles from Wendewende and was granted

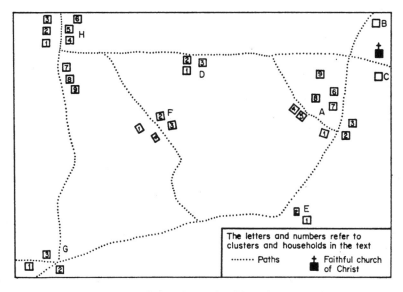

Fig. 2. Part of Wendewende village (not to scale)

a site in Wendewende village. The first Tapara died in 1956 and at that time his son Severe attempted to take over the position from him, but was unsuccessful. Village headman Wendwende insisted that the title went to a matrilineal relative. My contacts were based upon a relationship with Severe, and the conflict existing between him and the present Tapara explains why I have no details regarding the latter's household.

Severe was able to obtain land for the headquarters of the Faithful Church of Christ when his father was *nyakwawa* and he started the sect in 1950.

There are two clusters of nine houses (Clusters A and H on the map), one of four houses (Cluster F), two of three houses (Clusters D and G), one of two houses (Cluster E) and two single houses (B and C) in the area.

Cluster A

The genealogical ties of the inhabitants of this cluster are shown on Wendewende genealogy No. 1.

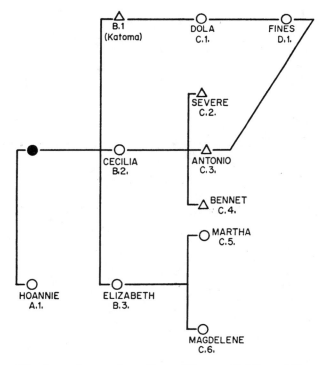

FIG. 3. Wendewende genealogy No. 1 (Cluster A) (C1 and D1 are linked patrilaterally to the remainder of the genealogy)

APPENDIX A

147

Household No. 1 consists of a simple primary family, comprising Severe (C2 on the genealogy) and his wife Cecilia and six children all of whom are living in the house. This house is a large brick one with several rooms, glass windows and a considerable quantity of European furniture, including a three-piece suite, carpet, beds etc. Later, after the time that the census upon which this analysis is based was taken, the house was extended so that it was well above the average standard, even for educated Africans, in the District. Near the house is a maize-mill belonging to Severe; this is a twin cylinder diesel model which was purchased new at a cost of over £250, and which does a thriving trade. Severe is recognized as *mwini mbumba* by all the people named on Genealogy No. 1, with the exception of Katoma's patrilineal descendants. Katoma is recognized as the real *mwini mbumba*, but he has now settled in Northern Rhodesia, and Severe is recognized as *mwini mbumba* for all practical purposes.

Severe married his wife, who is Nguru, virilocally; he did not transfer money to her family. As the leader of the Faithful Church of Christ, for which he receives financial support from the United States, Severe has considerable influence in the area. Attached to the household is a paid servant, whose main duty is the supervision of the maize mill, but who also helps to clean the house: he lives about a mile away. Severe's wife and children are all members of the Faithful Church of Christ.

Household No. 2 consists of a rejuvenated family, comprising Cecilia (B2), mother of Severe and her husband Edson. Cecilia is a widow by the death of Severe's father Chimenya, and married Edson—a widower. There are no children by this marriage. Edson has married Cecilia uxorilocally; he is Nguru. Both are members of the Faithful Church of Christ: Cecilia was a Roman Catholic before the foundation of her son's sect, and Edson was a member of the Providence Industrial Mission before marrying Cecilia.

House No. 3. There is no Household No. 3; the house numbered 3 on the diagram has been built to accommodate visitors to the Faithful Church of Christ. It is used mainly by church ministers attending meetings at the headquarters of the sect.

Household No. 4 consists of a simple primary family comprising Antonio (C3), a brother of Severe, and his wife Fines (D1) and two infant children. This house is of traditional wattle and daub construction, but is larger than average and has glass windows. Fines is a mother's brother's daughter's daughter of Antonio and the marriage between them is an intra-village one. Antonio, who has been educated up to Standard Three, is a pastor in the Faithful Church of Christ; before the foundation of the sect by his brother he was a Roman Catholic, and before that a member of the Jehovah's Witnesses. Fines was also a Roman Catholic but is now a member of the Faithful Church of Christ.

148   SECTARIANISM IN SOUTHERN NYASALAND

Household No. 5 comprises an aged widow, Hoannie (A1), a sister of Cecilia's mother and a mother's mother's sister of Severe and Antonio. The house is separated by barely two yards from that of Antonio, who is looking after her. Hoannie has two daughters living in another part of Wendewende village, but she prefers to live near Antonio whom she brought up as a child. Hoannie was a Roman Catholic but states that she is now a member of the Faithful Church of Christ.

Household No. 6 consists of a rejuvenated family comprising Elizabeth (B3) and her husband Mendolo, and two children of Elizabeth's former marriage, who are unmarried and sleep in a *gowelo*. Elizabeth is a sister of Cecilia, mother of Severe, whom she recognizes as *mwini mbumba*. She divorced her previous husband in 1943 and married the present one ten years later. The marriage is uxorilocal. Elizabeth has two daughters who are married and living in the hamlet, and two sons who have married uxorilocally. Both she and her husband have received a sub-standard education. Both are members of the Faithful Church of Christ, Elizabeth being a deaconess; she became a member on its foundation having previously been a Roman Catholic. Mendolo was also previously a Roman Catholic but was excommunicated for divorcing his former wife, and joined the Faithful Church of Christ on his second marriage.

Household No. 7 consists of a residual family comprising Martha (C5) and her infant daughter. Martha is divorced from her husband and appears to be suffering from some form of psychosis which, informants state, has developed within the last two years and which has rendered her incapable of looking after a household. She is now being looked after by her mother Elizabeth.

Household No. 8 consists of a simple primary family comprising Magdalene (C6), her husband, Mekias, and four children. Magdalene is the daughter of Elizabeth and thus a matrilateral parallel cousin of Severe whom she recognizes as *mwini mbumba*. She has married Mekias uxorilocally. Both Mekias and Magdelene are Roman Catholics, and Magdalene is the only person in the cluster who recognizes Severe as *mwini mbumba* but who is not a member of the Faithful Church of Christ. The three eldest of her four children attend a nearby Roman Catholic Mission School.

Household No. 9 consists of a residual family comprising Dola (C1) and her two unmarried children. She has been divorced twice. Dola is a matrilateral cross-cousin of Severe and recognizes her brother who has married uxorilocally in another part of Wendewende village as *mwini mbumba*. She has four children, a daughter Fines (D1) who is married to Antonio (C3), and a son who has married uxorilocally, and two unmarried daughters who are attending a nearby Roman Catholic School. Dola states that she herself is a Roman Catholic in spite of the fact that she has been divorced twice.

House B. This isolated house is occupied by a widow Munalayekha, who is living alone. She has recently moved into the area from Portuguese East Africa on the death of her husband, having followed her son Luciano, who married uxorilocally in Cluster H. She has no other relatives nearby and recognizes Luciano as *mwini mbumba*. Since having been given a site in the area she has become a member of the Faithful Church of Christ.

House C. This house is occupied by Medrick, a teacher in the school attached to the headquarters of the Faithful Church of Christ, and secretary of the sect. He has no gardens in the area and only lives in the house from Monday to Friday while he is working in Wendewende. He goes to his wife's village, about eight miles away, on a Friday evening and returns on a Monday morning. Medrick is Nguru, but is unrelated to anyone else in the area; he has merely come for employment. Although employed by the Faithful Church of Christ he is a member of the Church of Scotland, and states that he has no intention of changing. He has been educated to Standard Six.

Cluster D

Genealogy No. 2 shows the relationships between the inhabitants of this cluster. This pattern of relationships is complex and atypical of the area.

Household No. 1 consists of a rejuvenated family comprising Singatiya and Suwedi. Singatiya was the second wife of Napata, who had first married his patrilateral cross-cousin Erissa. Singatiya was a matri-

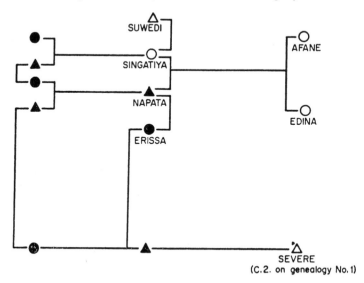

FIG. 4. Wendewende genealogy No. 2 (Cluster D) (Both consanguineal and affinal links are shown on this genealogy, which is atypical of the area)

150 SECTARIANISM IN SOUTHERN NYASALAND

lateral cross-cousin of Napata through a slave wife of his mother's brother. He was allowed therefore, to bring her to live virilocally. Both Napata and Erissa have now died, and Singatiya has married Suwedi who has moved to where Singatiya was previously living. Napata was a matrilateral cross-cousin of Severe's father Chimenya. Both Singatiya and Suwedi were members of the Faithful Church of Christ, but have now joined the Roman Catholic Church, stating that as Catholics they were allowed to brew beer.

Household No. 2 consists of a section of a compound family comprising Afane and her four children. She is the first wife of Mawindo, who spends half of his time with her and half with his other wife some twenty miles away. Afane is a daughter of the marriage between Napata and Singatiya. The marriage between Afane and Mawindo is based upon uxorilocal residence. Afane stated that she is a Roman Catholic, but that her husband is a pagan.

Household No. 3 consists of Edina who has recently divorced her husband Stephano and who is living alone, having no children. Edina is a daughter of the marriage between Napata and Singatiya. She is a member of the Faithful Church of Christ.

Cluster E

This cluster consists of two households unrelated to any other households in the area.

Household No. 1 consists of Felina, a widow living alone. She has been living at the present site since 1952, when she came with her brother who has since died. He came and begged land on which to settle after a dispute with some of his matrilineal relatives in a village some five miles away. Felina has no relatives nearby with the exception of her daughter Falis who lives in the adjacent house. She has three other daughters who have married uxorilocally in the village which she and her brother left. Felina is Nyanja and a member of the Faithful Church of Christ which she joined after she arrived in Wendewende, not having been a Christian before.

Household No. 2 consists of a simple primary family comprising Falis and her husband Hamsey and their three infant children. The marriage is uxorilocal, having taken place shortly after Falis moved to Wendewende with her mother Felina. Falis is Nyanja but Ramsey is Nguru. Both of them are members of the Church of Scotland, this being the only church or sect of which they have been members.

Cluster F

This cluster consists of four houses but despite repeated attempts it proved impossible to obtain details of the fourth household. This may have been due to the political situation at the time when the census was taken.

APPENDIX A 151

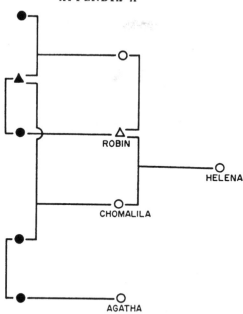

FIG. 5. Wendewende genealogy No. 3 (Cluster F)

Household No. 1 consists of a section of a residual compound family, comprising Robin and his second wife Chomalila; Robin's mother's brother had two wives and Robin has married a daughter of each of them. All the children of the marriage between Robin and Chomalila are now married and living elsewhere, with the exception of Helena who is married and living in the same cluster. Robin and his second wife moved into Wendewende some four years ago after having a disagreement with the village headman of their former village. They moved out of the village as an elementary family and were given a place in Wendewende. The eldest son of the marriage wanted to start a new village of his own, but Robin declined to live there. The son has not been able to establish a new village. Both Robin and Chomalila are Nyanja, neither of them is Christian.

Household No. 2 consists of a residual family comprising Helena, who has recently been divorced from her husband Garnett, and her two infant children. Being a daughter of Chomalila she is Nyanja; she recognizes her brother as *mwini mbumba*. She is a Roman Catholic.

Household No. 3 consists of Agatha, a widow, who is living alone. She is a matrilateral parallel cousin of Chomalila, and came to join her when her husband died. Chomalila is the only relative she has, apart from a son whom she recognizes as *mwini mbumba* and who is living and working in Limbe. Agatha is a Roman Catholic.

Cluster G

This cluster consists of three households, the relationship between the inhabitants of which are shown in Wendewende genealogy No. 4. The inhabitants of this cluster are related matrilaterally to the inhabitants of Cluster A. Asaina is a brother of the deceased *nyakwawa* Tapara, the father of Severe—the *mwini mbumba* of the dominant *mbumba* of Cluster A.

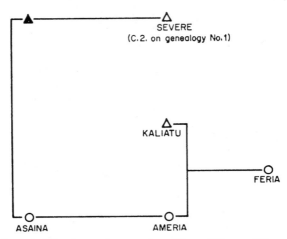

FIG. 6. Wendewende genealogy No. 4 (Cluster G)

Household No. 1 consists of a rejuvenated family comprising Asaina and her husband Robert. Asaina has one daughter by a previous husband; this daughter is also living in the cluster. After her divorce Asaina married Robert, an Nguru widower, uxorilocally. In the absence of any male matrilineal relatives in the area Asaina, an old woman and a great-grandmother, regards herself as *mwini mbumba*. Asaina is a Roman Catholic, Robert is not a Christian.

Household No. 2 consists of a rejuvenated family comprising Ameria, her husband Kaliatu, and one unmarried daughter of Ameria by a previous husband. Ameria is a daughter of Asaina, whom she recognizes as *mwini mbumba*; formerly she recognized the *nyakwawa* Tapara, her mother's brother, now deceased, as holding that position. She has divorced her first husband, and has married Kaliatu uxorilocally. She has one married daughter living in the cluster, another married daughter living with her husband who is working in Lilongwe, and a son who has married uxorilocally. Ameria is not a Christian; Kaliatu was a member of the Zambesi Industrial Mission, but was expelled for drinking beer.

Household No. 3 consists of a simple primary family comprising Feria, her husband Alan, and three infant children. Feria is the daughter of

APPENDIX A 153

Ameria and recognizes her mother's mother Asaina as *mwini mbumba*. She has married Alan uxorilocally. Alan comes from Zomba some fifty miles away and is employed outside the village during the week as a mattress-maker, but he usually spends the week-ends in Wendewende. Alan is Nyanja, though his wife is Nguru; he is a member of the Church of Scotland, whilst his wife is a member of the Faithful Church of Christ.

Cluster H

This cluster consists of nine houses, the relationships between the inhabitants of which are shown in Wendewende genealogy No. 5. There are three *mbumba* represented in this cluster and with one exception the grouping of the houses within the cluster reflects the matrilineal grouping of the female members of the households. The exception is Household No. 6, where Harry (D3) has married virilocally, and the position of the house reflects his matrilineal affiliation and not that of his wife. The female inhabitants of Houses Nos. 1, 2 and 3 are members of *mbumba* B on the diagram (in the case of House No. 1 Kasonya is a widower, but his deceased wife, Achipiri, was a member of this *mbumba*). These houses are separated from other houses of the cluster by a path. Houses Nos. 4 and 5 are inhabited by female members of *mbumba* A on the diagram, and separated from houses Nos. 7, 8 and 9, inhabited by female members of *mbumba* C, again by a path. All three *mbumba* are linked to the deceased *nyakwawa* Tapara by various links. *Mbumba* B was, before his death, part of Tapara's own *mbumba*, Achipiri having been his sister. *Mbumba* A is linked through the *mwini mbumba* Kasonya (B2) who is a matrilateral cross-cousin of Tapara, and who married Tapara's sister Achipiri. *Mbumba* C is linked to Tapara through the mother of Alieje (C8) and Alista (C6), who was a patrilateral cross-cousin of Tapara, the link between the two *mbumba* being strengthened by the marriage of Alista (C6) with her classificatory matrilateral cross-cousin Gideon (C5), who is now recognized as *mwini mbumba* of *mbumba* B.

Household No. 1 consists of Kasonya (B2) a widower living alone, but looked after by two of his married daughters who are living in adjacent houses. Kasonya has two unmarried daughters who are living with their married sisters Esteri (C3) and Theresa (C4). Kasonya is Nguru; he is not a Christian.

Household No. 2 consists of a simple primary family, comprising Esteri (C3) and her husband Joseph and one infant daughter. Esteri is a daughter of Kasonya and Achipiri; she has married Joseph uxorilocally and recognizes her brother Gideon (C5) as *mwini mbumba*. Both Esteri and Joseph are Nguru. Esteri was a member of the Faithful Church of Christ, but is no longer; similarly Joseph was a Roman Catholic, but no longer attends the church services.

S.S.N.–L

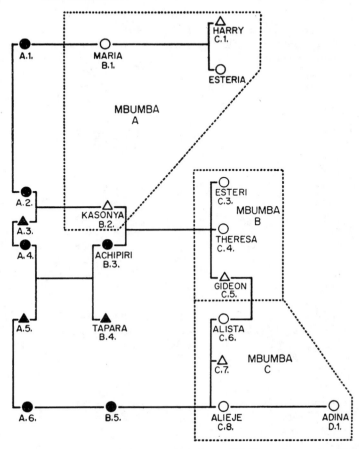

Fig. 7. Wendewende genealogy No. 5 (Cluster H) (In order to simplify this diagram the relative positions of siblings do not indicate relative age)

Household No. 3 consists of a simple primary family comprising Theresa (C4) and her husband. Theresa is a daughter of Kasonya and recognises Gideon as her *mwini mbumba*.

Household No. 4 consists of a rejuvenated family comprising Maria (B1) and her husband Kwelekwe. Maria is a matrilateral parallel cousin of Kasonya whom she recognizes as *mwini mbumba*. She was a widow when she married Kwelekwe a widower, uxorilocally. The two children of her former marriage are living in adjacent houses. Maria states that she is a Roman Catholic, while her husband is a member of the Church of Scotland.

Household No. 5 consists of a simple primary family comprising Esteria

APPENDIX A   155

and her husband Luciano and three small children. Esteria is a daughter of
Maria and recognizes Kasonya as *mwini mbumba*. She has married Luciano
uxorilocally; Luciano is Nguru, and his mother has recently moved into a
house in Wendewende (House B), having followed her son from Portuguese East Africa on the death of her husband. Both Luciano and Esteria
are Roman Catholics.

Household No. 6 consists of a simple primary family comprising Harry
(C1), his wife Aline and six unmarried children, the eldest of whom are
living in a *gowelo*. Harry is the son of Maria and recognizes Kasonya, his
mother's sister's son as *mwini mbumba*. He has married virilocally in the
knowledge that he will succeed to the position of *mwini mbumba* on the
death of Kasonya, who is now an old man. He has married his mother's
brother's daughter. Both Harry and Aline are Nguru, both of them are also
Roman Catholics, and their two eldest children are pupils at a local Roman
Catholic mission school.

Household No. 7 consists of a simple primary family, comprising Alieje
(C8), her husband Greyson, and four unmarried children. They have three
other children, two sons who are both in Salisbury, and a married daughter
in an adjacent household. Alieje is Nguru, but Greyson is Nyanja; the
marriage is uxorilocal. Greyson receives a monthly pension from the
Government in compensation for wounds which he received as a member
of the King's African Rifles. He is educated up to Standard One and has
served in India and Siam. Alieje recognizes a brother living in another part
of Wendewende village as *mwini mbumba*. Both Alieje and Greyson are
Roman Catholics, as are all their children with the exception of Adina
(D1). They have all been, or are being educated, in Roman Catholic schools,
one of their sons having reached Standard Four.

Household No. 8 consists of a temporary residual potential family.
Adina (D1) is living alone. Her husband Damson is in the King's African
Rifles and stationed in Northern Rhodesia. Adina recognizes her mother's
brother as *mwini mbumba*. Both Adina and Damson are members of the
Church of Scotland, Adina was formerly a Roman Catholic, but joined the
Church of Scotland to marry Damson, who was already a member of
that Church.

Household No. 9 consists of a simple primary family comprising Alista
(C6), her husband Gideon (C5), and three young daughters, under the age
of puberty. This is an intra-cluster marriage, but the house is situated
adjacent to Alista's sister's house. Alista and Gideon are classificatory
cross-cousins; both are Nguru. Gideon is *mwini mbumba* over his four
sisters and is living close to them. Alista recognizes a brother living in
another section of the village as *mwini mbumba*. Both Gideon and Alista are
Roman Catholics, and their two eldest daughters are attending a local
Roman Catholic mission school.

APPENDIX B

This poem is the Introduction to a tract called 'Proof', sent from a Church of Christ in the United States to the Faithful Church of Christ.

(Read first letter of each line for title of Poem.)

Sunday School is like a tree,
Under which men like to be,
Never doubting what is taught
Division is by Satan brought,
All trees are known by fruits they bear,
You see my friend what kind is here.

Such fruits, won't you stop and think?
Cannot please God but soon must sink,
How deep my friends no one can tell,
One thing we know a place called hell,
Old Satan is the captain there,
Look out for trees by fruits they bear.

For when earth's millions shall appear,
Remember what I tell you here,
Unto God's word account we'll give
In which no Sunday School does live,
Therein is found no Sunday School,
So who on earth now is the fool?

Surely friends you will agree,
As these truths I offer thee,
To the Bible all must go,
And by this fact the truth we know,
Nowhere in Scripture will you find
Sunday School to be devine, (sic)

What old Satan likes to do, is
Everywhere divide the pew,
And what he'll use to make success,
Poor deluded folks like the best:
One thing I know, by Heaven's rule,
No Church will have the Sunday School.

BIBLIOGRAPHY OF WORKS CITED IN THE TEXT

Andersson, E., *Messianic Popular Movements in the Lower Congo*. Uppsala and Stockholm, 1958.
Atkins, G. 'The Nyanja-speaking Population of Nyasaland and Northern Rhodesia.' *African Studies*, Vol. 9, No. 1, March 1950. pp. 35–39.

Balandier, G. 'Messianismes et Nationalismes en Afrique Noire.' *Cahiers Internationaux de Sociologie*, Vol. 14, 1953. pp. 41–65.
Banton, M. 'An Independent Church in Sierra Leone.' *Hibbert Journal*, Vol. LV, 1954, pp. 555–60.
Banton, M. 'Adaptation and Integration in the Social System of Temne Immigrants in Freetown.' *Africa*, Vol. XXVI, 1956, pp. 354–67.
Barnes, J. A. 'The Fort Jameson Ngoni.' In Gluckman, M., and Colson, E., *Seven Tribes of British Central Africa*, London, 1950.
Barnes, J. A. *Politics in a Changing Society*. Cape Town, 1954.
Barnes, J. A. 'Seven Types of Segmentation.' *Rhodes-Livingstone Journal*, Vol. XVII, 1955.
Bettison, D. G. 'The Social and Economic Structure of Seventeen Villages— Blantyre/Limbe, Nyasaland.' *Rhodes-Livingstone Communication*. Lusaka, 1958.
Bettison, D. G. 'Migrancy and Social Structure in Peri-Urban Communities in Nyasaland.' In *Present Inter-relations in Central African Rural and Urban Life*. Proceedings of the 11th Conference of the Rhodes-Livingstone Institute, 1958.
Bruwer, J. 'Kinship Terminology among the Cewa of the Eastern Province of Northern Rhodesia.' *African Studies*, Vol. 7, 1948, pp. 185–7.

Carstairs, E. M. 'The View from the Shrine.' *The Listener*, 2 March, 1961.
Cohn, N. *The Pursuit of the Millennium*. 1957.
Colson, E. *Marriage and the Family among the Plateau Tonga of Northern Rhodesia*. Manchester, 1958.
Cunnison, I. 'The Watch-Tower Assembly in Central Africa.' *International Review of Missions*, Vol. 40, 1951.

Devlin, P. (Chairman). *Report of the Nyasaland Commission of Enquiry*. 1959.
Duckworth, E. H. 'A Visit to the Apostles and the Town of Aiyetoro.' *Nigeria*, 36, 1951, p. 387–442.
Dynes, R. 'Church-Sect Typology and Socio-Economic Status.' *American Sociological Review*, 1955. pp. 555–60.

Evans-Pritchard, E. E. *Witchcraft, Oracles and Magic among the Azande*. Oxford, 1937.
Evans-Pritchard, E. E. *The Nuer*. Oxford, 1940.

Field, M. J. *Search for Security*. London, 1960.
Firth, R. 'Problem and Assumption in an Anthropological Study of Religion.' *Journal of the Royal Anthropological Institute*, Vol. 89, No. 2, 1959.
Fortes, M. *The Web of Kinship among the Tallensi*. London, 1949.

Gerth, H. H., and Mills, C. W. *From Max Weber—Essays in Sociology*. 1948.
Gluckman, M. 'Kinship and Marriage among the Lozi of Northern Rhodesia and the Zulu of Natal.' In Radcliffe-Brown, A. R., and Forde, D., *African Systems of Kinship and Marriage*. London, 1950.
Graves, R., *Lars Porsena*. London, 1927.

158 SECTARIANISM IN SOUTHERN NYASALAND

Hanna, A. J. *The Beginnings of Nyasaland and North-Eastern Rhodesia, 1859–95.* Oxford, 1956.

Hastings, J. (ed.). *Encyclopaedia of Religion and Ethics.* 1908.

Hobsbawm, E. J., *Primitive Rebels.* Manchester, 1959.

Johnston, Sir H. H. *British Central Africa.* London, 1897.

Köbben, A. J. F. 'Prophetic Movements as an Expression of Social Protest.' *International Archives of Ethnology*, Vol. 49, 1960. pp. 138–63.

Kuper, H. *An African Aristocracy.* London, 1947.

Leakey, L. S. B. *Mau-Mau and the Kikuyu.* London, 1952.

Leakey, L. S. B. *Defeating Mau-Mau.* London, 1954.

Linton, R. 'Nativistic Movements.' *American Anthropologist*, Vol. 45, No. 3. 1943.

Livingstone, D. *Narrative of an Expedition to the Zambesi and its Tributaries 1858–1864.* London, 1865.

MacDonald, D. *Africana—the Heart of Heathen Africa.* London, 1882.

Malekebu, B. *Makolo Athu.* Zomba, 1949.

Marwick, M. G. 'The Social Context of Cewa Witch Beliefs.' *Africa*, Vol. XXII, 1952. pp. 120–34, 215–33.

Marwick, M. G. 'The Kinship Basis of Cewa Social Structure.' *South African Journal of Science*, March, 1952. pp. 258–62.

McCulloch, M. *The Southern Lunda and Related Peoples.* International African Institute. Ethnographic Survey, West Central Africa, Part I, 1949.

Mitchell, J. C. 'The Political Organization of the Yao of Southern Nyasaland.' *African Studies*, Vol. VIII, No. 3, 1949. pp. 141–59.

Mitchell, J. C. *The Yao Village.* Manchester, 1956.

Mqotsi, L. and Mkele, N. *A Separatist Church Ibandla Lika Krestu*, African Studies, 1946.

Murray, S. S. (compiler). *A Handbook of Nyasaland.* Government Printer, Zomba, 1932.

Nadel, S. F. *A Black Byzantium.* London, 1942.

Nash, P. 'The Place of Religious Revivalism in the Formation of the Inter-Cultural Community on the Klamath Reservation.' In Eggan, F., *Social Anthropology of the North American Tribes*, 1955. pp. 377–444.

Ngwane, H. D. *Some Aspects of Marriage in Peri-Urban Villages in Blantyre/Limbe.* Rhodes-Livingstone Communication No. 17, 1959.

Nyasaland Government. *Census Report for Nyasaland, 1945.* Government Printer, Zomba, 1946.

Parrinder, G. *Religion in An African City.* London, 1953.

Pauw, B. A. *Religion in a Tswana Chiefdom.* London, 1960.

Platt, W. J. *An African Prophet.* London, 1934.

Pope, L. *Millhands and Preachers.* New Haven, 1942.

Porter, Arthur T. 'Religious Affiliation in Freetown, Sierra Leone.' *Africa*, Vol. XXIII, 1953. pp. 3–14.

Rangeley, W. H. J. 'Nyau' in Kota-Kota District.' *Nyasaland Journal*, Vol. II, No. 2, July 1949 and Vol. II, No. 2, July, 1950.

Richards, A. I. 'Reciprocal Clan Relationships among the Bemba.' *Man*, Vol. XXXVII, 1937. Article 122.

Richards, A. I. *Land, Labour and Diet in Northern Rhodesia.* London, 1939.

Rotberg, R. 'The Lenshina Movement of Northern Rhodesia,' *Human Problems in British Central Africa*, xxix, June 1961. pp. 63–78.

BIBLIOGRAPHY OF WORKS CITED IN THE TEXT 159

Schapera, I. *Government and Politics in Tribal Societies*. London, 1956.
Schapera, I. *The Tswana*. International African Institute, Ethnographic Survey. Southern Africa. Part III, 1953.
Schlosser, K. *Eingeborenenkirchen in Süd- und Südwestafrika*. Kiel, 1958.
Scott, C., and Hetherwick, A. *Dictionary of the Nyanja Language*. 1929.
Shepperson, G. 'The Politics of African Church Separatist Movements in British Central Africa 1892–1916. *Africa*, Vol. XXIV, 1954. pp. 233–47.
Shepperson, G., and Price, T. *Independent African*. Edinburgh, 1958.
Smith, M. W. 'Towards a Classification of Cult Movements.' *Man*, lix, 2, Jan. 1959. pp. 8–12.

Stacey, M. *Tradition and Change—A Study of Banbury*. 1960.
Stefaniszyn, B. 'Funeral Friendship in Central Africa.' *Africa*, Vol. XX, No. 4, 1950. pp. 290–306.
Sundkler, B. G. M. *Bantu Prophets in South Africa*, (2nd ed.) London, 1961.

Taylor, J. V. *Processes of Growth in an African Church*. London, 1958.
Taylor, J. V., and Lehmann, D. *Christians of the Copper-Belt*. London, 1961.

Wach, J. *The Sociology of Religion*. 1947.
Wallace, A. F. C., 'Revitalization Movements', *American Anthropologist*, lviii, 1956, pp. 264–81.
Ward, Barbara E. 'Some Observations on Religious Cults in Ashanti.' *Africa*, Vol. XXVIII, 1956. pp. 47–60.
Watson, W. *Tribal Cohesion in a Money Economy*. Manchester, 1957.
Welbourn, F. *East African Rebels*. London, 1961.
Werner, A. *The Native Tribes of British Central Africa*. London, 1906.
Wilson, M. *Communal Rituals of the Nyakyusa*. London, 1959.
Wishlade, R. L. 'Chiefship and Politics in the Mlanje District of Southern Nyasaland.' *Africa*, Vol. XXXI, No. 1, 1961. pp. 36–45.
Worsley, P. *And the Trumpet Shall Sound*. 1957.

Yinger, J. M. *Religion, Society and the Individual*. New York, 1957.
Young, T. C. 'The Meaning of the Word "Family".' *Man*, Vol. XXXI, 1931. Article 126.

INDEX

Adzukulu, 61
African Church Crucified Mission, 11, 24, 64
African Church of Christ, 18, 24, 33, 34, 38, 71, 83, 110, 128
African Greek Orthodox Church, 4, 134, 140–1
African National Congress, 41, 94–98
African Nyasa Church, 20, 24, 37, 71, 81, 106, 133
African United Baptist Church, 20, 24
Africanism, 40, 50
Agriculture, 122
Alexander, Archbishop, 141
Ancestor cult, 137–8
Ancestral spirits, 48
Anglican Church, 131, 134, 141
Anglican missionaries, 10
Apartheid, 40, 41
'Apostolic Succession', 35, 62, 74, 75, 98, 140
Assemblies of God, 11, 24, 36, 55, 56, 107, 109

Banda, Dr. H., 42–43, 91
Bamalaki, 4, 134
Baptism, 36, 45, 57, 58, 67, 110, 126, 127
Baptist Industrial Mission, 14, 36
Beer-drinking, 49
Bettison, D., 102
Bible, 45, 49, 55, 62, 83, 135, 136
Blantyre, 11, 16, 31–32, 102, 123, 129, 130, 131, 134
Booth, J., 12ff., 17, 124, 127
British Churches of Christ, 15, 71

Cargo cults, 42n.
Cewa, 81
Chapananga's area, 6ff., 16, 22, 25, 26, 123, 129, 130, 143
Chateka, J., 17–18, 38, 39–40, 71
Chiefship, 76–79, 86, 88, 89
Chikwawa District, 5ff., 16, 78, 86, 89, 90
Chilembwe, J., 2, 15–16, 17, 71, 134, 135, 138, 139
Chilembwe Rising, 17, 135, 137
Cholo District, 20, 91
Church buildings, 31, 53, 122
Church 'dues', 123–4

Church of Central Africa (Presbyterian), 11n., 33, 69, 70
Church of Christ in Africa, 18, 24
Church of God, 18, 24, 34, 110
Church of the Nazarene, 34, 109
Churches of Christ, 17
Cikunda, 6, 28
Clerks, 63
Congregations, numbers of, 23–25, 105
Congregations, size of, 25–26, 126

'Descendants of Ham' Doctrine, 40, 51–52
Disputes, arbitration of, 67, 79, 87, 88
District Administration (Natives) Ordinance 1912, 85
Divorce, 112–13, 114

Ecclesiastical Courts, 118–19
Ecumenical movements, 37
Education standards, 65. 68, 70, 71, 93, 99, 124, 132–3
Ethiopian Church, 20–21, 24, 33–34, 46–52, 61, 73–74, 81, 92, 94, 97, 116–17, 135, 136, 138
Ethiopianism, 51–52, 135
Eucharist, 56
Expulsion from congregations, 110, 111

Faithful Church of Christ, 18–19, 24, 33, 37, 39, 56, 57, 59, 61, 63, 66, 70, 81, 82–83, 106, 107, 108, 109, 110, 111, 118, 120–1, 128, 145–55
Faith-healing, 45, 137
Federation of Rhodesia and Nyasaland, 95, 97, 98
Fishing, 122–3
Free Church of Scotland, 11, 63
Funeral rites, 59, 61, 126

Ghost Dances, 42n.
Gluckman, M., 114n.

Healing Sects, 45
Hobsbawm, E. J., 42
Household composition, 145–55
Hymnbooks, 38, 50

Initiation ceremonial, 30
Islam, 31, 41, 143, 144

INDEX

Jehovah's Witnesses, 43–44

Kagulu ka Nkhosa, 19–20, 24, 34, 37, 62, 71, 124
Kantini, 123
Kenya, 129, 135, 142
Kimbangism, 138

Land, rights over, 68
Lenshina, A., 45
Linton, R., 46
Livingstone, D., 10ff.
Lord's Prayer, 44
Lundu Chief, 76

Magomero, 10, 17
Makwinja, A., 17, 38, 71
Malawi Party, 30
Malekebu, Dr. D., 17, 70, 72, 133
Mass, 56, 99
Marriage, 102–3, 112–13
Marriage Ordinance, 59
Matrilineally linked family groups, 28
Mau-Mau, 135
Mbumba, 7, 77, 78, 79, 103, 105, 145–55
Messianism, 42–45, 129, 138–40
Mikalongwe Mission, 21, 36, 70
Millenarianism, 42–45
Mitchell, J. C., 80
Mlanje District, 5ff., 11, 12, 22–27, 77, 78, 80, 81, 86, 89, 90, 101, 102, 104, 105, 123, 129, 130, 143, 145
Mobility between sects, 83, 100, 110, 111, 116
Montfarist Marist Fathers, 11
Mtnudu, 27
Mwini Dziko, 48, 77, 86, 92–94, 127
Mwini Mbumba, 7, 48, 78, 79, 80, 82, 103–4, 112, 113

Native Authorities, 29, 85–89
Native Authority Courts, 51, 91–92
Native Authority Ordinance 1933, 8, 85–86
Nazombe, Native Authority, 48, 77, 86, 93–94, 113, 114
Ngonde, 132
Ngoni, 31, 108, 137, 138
Nguru, 6, 28–31, 50, 89–91, 107, 108, 138
Northern Rhodesia, 130
Ntepha, 48, 74, 77, 92, 95
Nyakwawa, 7, 86–87, 88, 92, 145, 146

Nyakyusa, 132
Nyambo, P., 20, 47
Nyanja, 6, 27–31, 89–91, 108, 134, 138
Nyanja language, 29–30, 50, 108
Nyasa Industrial Mission, 14, 20;, 24, 36, 70

Old Testament, 47, 48

Pauw, B. A., 76, 136–7, 143
Pentecostal Holiness Church, 19, 109
Phombeya, 20, 81
Political system, 76–92
Political units, formation of, 77–80
Polygyny, 115, 116, 120
Population density, 89–91, 124, 130
Population migrations, 27–29, 84, 85, 89, 91, 105
Portuguese East Africa, 27
Principle of Primacy, 77, 79
Prophets, 42–45, 70, 139
Providence Industrial Mission, 2, 15–16, 17, 20, 24, 30–31, 32, 65, 66, 70, 122, 135, 139

Revivalism, 55, 56
'Rite de passage', 58
Roman Catholic Church, 3, 11, 24, 25, 31, 33, 35, 43, 55, 56

Sanctions, 117–19
Schapera, I., 133
Schools, 103, 106–7, 121, 122, 136
Scotland, Church of, 3, 11, 16, 24, 25, 31, 33, 39, 41, 55, 57, 65, 66, 67, 68, 82, 83, 102, 106, 110, 119, 127,(134
Second Coming of Christ, 43
Sena, 113
Sent of the Holy Ghost Church, 19, 24, 34, 37, 109
Sermons, 54–56
Seventh-day Adventists, 14–15, 20, 24, 33, 36, 44, 53
Seventh-day Baptists, 14–15, 17–18, 24, 33, 36, 38, 53, 63, 135, 136
Severe, E. C., 18, 66–67, 70–71, 72, 81, 104–5, 118, 133, 145–55
Settlement pattern, 101, 102, 105, 125, 145–55
Shepperson, G., & Price, T., 12–17, 20, 134, 135, 136
Shire Highlands, 32, 130, 131
Shire Valley, 10, 16

162   INDEX

Simple secessionist sects, 4
Smith, M., 46
Socio-economic class, 132–33
Sons of God, 18, 24, 34, 38, 71, 128
Spirit possession, 138
Standards of living, 72
Stipends, 67–68, 69, 119
Struggle for office, 80, 81
Succession to ecclesiastical office, 73
Sundkler, B. G. M., 40
Swazi, 132, 134

Tswana, 133, 137, 143

Uganda, 129, 133, 134, 140–2
Undi, 27, 76
Uniforms, 127
United States, 34, 72, 82, 109, 110, 124, 139
Universities' Mission to Central Africa, 10, 101

Unkhoswe, 64, 112, 113

Village composition, 29
Village headmen, 29, 78–80, 84, 86–89, 93, 94

Wage labour, 123
Watch Tower, 3, 15, 24, 36, 43–44
Welbourn, F. B., 129, 134, 140, 143
Wendewende Village, 72, 87, 45–55
Witchcraft accusations, 81

Yao, 6, 27–31, 89, 91, 134, 138
Yinger, J. M., 2

Zambesi Industrial Mission, 12–14, 16, 19, 24, 36, 70, 119
Zionist Sects, 45, 132, 134, 135, 137
Zomba District, 20, 57, 66
Zululand, 45, 46, 136, 137